Tim Chipps

Make America Right Again

The War on Culture

Also by Tim Chipps

Ominous Alliance

Gross Injustice

National Preservation
or
National Perversion

Citizens Handbook

Follyhood

Published exclusively by
Artisan Vintage Works

Printed in the United States of America

To contact us or order our publications,
please visit our website:
www.artisanvintageworks.com

Dedication

To all American Patriots whose service and sacrifice makes it possible for us to live in freedom and peace as one nation under God.

In loving memory of our children Seva and Matthew.

Acknowledgments and special thanks to all those who contributed to the content of this book in excerpts, quotes, photos and advice.

Index

Introduction

In reading this book, you will embark on a journey in time, back to the early beginnings of American History in the year 1776, providing the reader the opportunity to visit briefly and understand a clearer insight into the hearts and minds of famous American leaders and presidents, who blazed the trail of our great nation. You will witness what these leaders believed and thought as they paved the road and path to freedom.

In the chapters that follow, you can examine the issues that face our country today and arrive at your own conclusion as to what truly made America great and what must be done to ensure that this precious heritage of liberty be passed onto our children, and to all generations yet to come. There is clearly a sense of polarization that exists in American culture. The diametric opposition in views politically, philosophically and intellectually vary substantially-- Liberal progressives on the left and traditional conservative ideology on the right.

I have attempted to be transparent but subjective and honest in presenting the arguments and debate on the main topic of culture, because it is relative to the issues and views expressed on either side.

I hope you will be inspired and encouraged as the pages of history continue to unfold and we tell the story of America with our lives and actions.

Chapter 1
A Nation Is Born

It was a famous day in history, the year 1776. America declared its independence from the British. A nation is born, America, a new country would soon be forged, as the patriots entered into the Revolutionary War against the British. The colonists came to this new world with a dream and vision of freedom. Since the early 1700's they were under the oppression of the British rulers. In 1788 the revolution was over and the American patriots emerged victorious.

The founding fathers, now faced with the great task of governing this new republic, would require the collective participation of all its citizens in developing a new government. This challenge engaged much debate and consideration, as the system of self-governance was carefully crafted. After many revisions were made, an extraordinary document was drafted. The Constitution was adapted in 1789. This monumental instrument would be the foundation by which the American system of self-governance would be built. Its content specifically described the fundamental laws and principles prescribed in the nature, functions, and limitations of power for the new republic. Its author's primary focus and purpose, intending to limit the role of government, assuring and affirming the guarantee of freedom and equality to all the citizens of this new nation.

Samuel Adams, cousin of John Adams, (second president), was a notable figure during this period. As a distinguished statesman and governor

Samuel Adams

of Massachusetts, he earned a widely respected reputation as an influential founding father throughout the Republic. In a letter he admonished all members of the new society: *"A general dissolution of principles and values will more surely overthrow the liberties of America more so than the whole force of the common enemy. If the people remain virtuous, they cannot be subdued, but when once they loose their virtue, will be ready to surrender their liberties to the first internal or external invader. If knowledge and values are diffused among the people, they will never be enslaved. This will be their great security."*

This profound statement transcends time, applying to all the future generations of Americans yet to live. The vast majority of Americans were devoted to Judeo-Christian principles and faith, deriving their virtues and morality from biblical teaching and inspiration.

In the following chapters we will attempt to examine and uncover what has happened in America's culture. In a step by step, systematic process, there has been an assault upon our virtues, launched by sources of radical left wing liberals, who aspire to and promote atheist and secular humanist views. Their goal is to remove any influence of bible based principles once taught in every public school. Their efforts have been consequential in tearing down traditional values and character development in American society.

Chapter 2 War on Culture

Education and the Supreme Court

The author's goal and theme of this book is to inspire hope in people's hearts and minds for America's future. It is possible to reverse the trend of degeneracy rampant in our culture. If we willingly participate in demanding positive change from our elected officials who support conservative traditional values in schools, work place and public forum; If we stand together and take an active role in reversing this trend, it can result in the restoration of America's conscience and integrity. If we do nothing, the tide of complicity will rise and the erosion will continue until nothing is left but anarchy.

"If we ever forget that we are one nation under God, then we will be a nation gone under."
(President Ronald Reagan)

Photo: Ronald Reagan Library

President Ronald Reagan

"America will never be destroyed from the outside. If we falter and loose our freedoms it will be because we destroyed ourselves."
(President Abraham Lincoln.)

The theory of evolution introduced by Charles Darwin is the only source of explanation for human origin taught in public schools and colleges since 1965. On his death bed, Darwin is quoted as saying, *"I regret that I suggested a theory and that gullible men gobbled it up as though it were a fact. I never intended that."* If by some we are considered mere animals and beast of nature, rather than the creation of God, we are to be pitied eternally.

"A fool says in his heart, there is no God."
(Psalm 14: 1-2)

The fallen nature of man is a result of choices each person takes as they journey through life. If the spirit of man can be regenerated through his relationship with his Creator, then the creationist view is confirmed to be substantiated. If men choose to remain isolated on a path, apart from God, their fallen nature will eventually cause the collapse of reason and purpose from within, and his tendencies will become beastly in conduct.

"To educate a man in mind and not in morals, is to educate a menace to society"
(President Theodore Roosevelt)

"With the demise of the biblical religions, that have provided the American core values since their country's inception, we are reverting to the world

Photo Library of Congress

President Theodore Roosevelt

6

pagan view. Trees and animals are venerated, while man is simply one more animal in the ecosystem and largely a hindrance, not an asset." (Dennis Prager)

A hallmark of the liberal atheist leader, Madalyn Murry O'Hair, was her instrumental role in removing bible reading in America's classrooms through the Supreme Court lawsuit in 1963. One year later, the supreme court decision was made to officially prohibit prayer in public schools. In 1964, Life Magazine featured her as "The most hated woman in America".

It has been half a century since this action took place. Five generations of Americans going to school without any influence of Judeo Christian values being taught in American classrooms.

Secular humanist and atheist groups, such as .A.C.L.U., i.e. American Civil Liberties Union, are on an all out quest in their agenda to remove nativity scenes, displays of the ten commandments or any other reference to biblical religion throughout the public view. Every symbol of faith is on their list, from the excerpt "one nation under God", a phrase in the Pledge of Allegiance, to the statement "in God we trust" printed on our currency. Their determination has been relentless in the "Godless society" they hope to establish.

Amazingly, only 3% of America's population consists of self proclaimed atheists, where as 76% of the American population, a staggering 240 million people, profess their faith and allegiance to the God of the Bible. How did this happen? What can we do? Face it, Christians have become complacent and passive. If there is to be any hope for positive change, we must actively do our part to fight back against the outrageous bias of hypocrisy displayed from radical left wing liberals. It is disgraceful!

What would happen if three quarters of the total population in America would gather in public sentiment, protesting to the injustice that has occurred in the attempt from minorities to rob us of our heritage? We need to hold accountable judges in the highest court who, in presumption, pretend to be the very conscience of the American people, and thereby legislate unconstitutional hear-says from their benches as if they were kings on thrones.

The virtuous chief justice, Potter Stewart, dissented from the decision to remove biblical teaching and prayer from school classrooms, blasting the ruling, and stating, *"It leads not to neutrality with respect to religion, but the establishment of secularism."* Education is the act or process of imparting knowledge. In the guise of neutrality, children are taught the theory of evolution as if it were the true origin of life, when in fact, it is only a presumptive theory. This position leaves no option for the creation of God in the learning process.

"We the people are the rightful masters of both Congress and the Courts, not to overthrow the constitution, but to overthrow the people who pervert the constitution." (President Abraham Lincoln)

"To compel a man to furnish funds for the propagation of ideas he disbelieves and abhors, is sinful and tyrannical. I have sworn upon the altar of

God, eternal hostility against every form of tyranny over the mind of man". (President Thomas Jefferson)

In order to be certain of the necessary corrective changes that must be made to protect our freedoms, we must participate. Voting at the ballot box is crucial. Our elected officials expect to hear from us, as their constituents, regarding these legislative issues. By writing and calling your U.S. congressmen and senators, we can together effect change by implementing consensus. If we unite and actively participate in the process of self governance, we can suggest to our lawmakers to propose and enact a constitutional amendment, clarifying protection of religious rights inherent to our constitution, guaranteeing freedom of expression and allowing the voluntary exercise of bible instruction and prayer in public schools, and protection of religious symbolism in the public domain.

Jesus said, "Let the little children come to me and do not hinder them, for the kingdom of heaven belongs to such as these." (Mt. 19:14)

"Hear, O Israel. The Lord our God, the Lord is one. Love the Lord your God with all your heart, and with all your soul, and with all your strength. These commandments that I give you today are to be upon your hearts. Impress them on your children. Talk about them when you get up." (Dt.6:4-7)

"For attaining wisdom and discipline; for understanding words of insight; for acquiring a disciplined and prudent life, doing what is right, just and fair; for giving prudence to the simple, knowledge

and discretion to the young–Let the wise listen and add to their learning, and let the discerning get guidance." (Pr. 1:1-5—Proverbs of Solomon, son of David, King of Israel)

The precious truth of God's word is what made noble the men and women who founded our great country. To disregard the wisdom and knowledge of God, is to embrace the foolishness and ignorance of man.

"Our constitution was made only for a moral and religious people. It is wholly inadequate to the government of any other." (President John Adams)

"The Hebrew have done more to civilize men than any other nation: The doctrine of a supreme intelligent sovereign of the universe, I believe to be the great essential principle of all morality, and consequently of all civilization." (President John Adams)

"Freedom is never more that one generation away from extinction. We did not pass it on to our children in the blood stream. It must be fought for, protected and handed on for them to do the same." (President Ronald Reagan)

"Within the covers of the bible, are the answers for all the problems we face." (President Ronald Reagan)

"Freedom prospers when religion is vibrant and the rule or law under God is acknowledged." (President Ronald Reagan)

"Without God, democracy will not, and cannot endure." (President Ronald Reagan)

On virtue: "No nation deserves to exist, if it permits itself to lose the stern and virile virtues; and this without regard to whether the loss is due to the growth of a heartless and all absorbing commercialism, to prolonged indulgence in luxury and soft effortless ease, or to the defecation of a warped and twisted sentimentality."
(President Theodore Roosevelt)

"A thorough knowledge of the bible is worth more than a college education."
(President Theodore Roosevelt)

"Our leaders must remember that education doesn't begin with some isolated bureaucrat in Washington. It doesn't even begin with state or local officials. Education begins in the home, where it is a parental right and responsibility."
(President Ronald Reagan)

"Parents train up a child in the way he should go, and when he is old, he will not depart from it."
(Proverbs 22:6)

"To those who cite the first amendment as reason for excluding God from the home and more of our institutions, and everyday life, may I just say… the first amendment of the constitution was not written to protect the people of this country from religious values. It was written to protect religious values from government tyranny." (President Ronald Reagan)

"When our founding fathers passed the first amendment, they sought to protect churches from government interference. They never intended to construct a wall of hostility between government and the concept of religious belief itself."
(President Ronald Reagan)

Politics and morality are inseparable and, as morality's foundation is religion, religion and politics are necessarily related. We need religion as a guide. We need it because we are imperfect, and our government needs the church, because only those humble enough to admit they're sinners can bring to democracy the tolerance it requires in order to survive." (President Ronald Reagan)

"The Declaration of Independence and the Constitution of the United States are concerns we have made, not only with ourselves, but with all mankind. Our founding documents proclaim to the world that freedom is not the sole prerogative of a chosen few. It is the universal right of all God's children." (President Ronald Reagan)

Homosexuality

The only reference notable in history pertaining to homosexuality promoted by a nation or society is found in the cities of Sodom and Gomorrah, including the world's destruction during the time of the flood. Both of these historical accounts are found in the bible in which God's word explicitly warns people not to engage in this immoral behavior.

"Because of this God gave them over to shameful lusts. Even their women had exchanged natural sexual relations with women and were inflamed with lust for one another. Men committed shameful acts with other men, and received in themselves the due penalty for their error.
(Romans 1:26-27)

"The general principles on which the fathers achieved independence were the general principles of Christianity. I will avow that I then believed, and now believe, that those general principles of Christianity are as eternal and imitable as the existence and attributes of God." (President John Adams)

"If ever the time should come, when vain and aspiring men shall possess the highest seat in government, our country will stand in need of its experienced patriots to prevent its ruin."
(Founding Father Samuel Adams)

Abortion

Abortion is clearly the unconscionable act of barbaric brutality and slaughter of an unborn child. If a woman chooses to engage in this act, let it be upon her own head, but for the Supreme Court to advocate legislative approval for the mass murder and funding of this whole scale atrocity, it is terroristic in nature, and the most evil of indulgence on behalf of God's creation. Judges who presume to dictate in choosing who will die or who will live is an act in which God

Janet R. Chipps

The term "fetus" comes from the Latin word meaning "young one."

himself would not engage. Not since Nazi Germany have so many innocent lives been taken. In truth, it is likened to the holocaust where 6 million Jews were slaughtered. The Supreme Court decision of Roe vs. Wade allowing U.S. taxpayers to fund this horrific act must be overturned.

"And there is the matter of abortion. We must, with calmness and resolve, help the vast majority of our fellow Americans understand that the more than 1.6 million abortions performed in America in 1980, amount to a great moral evil, an assault on the sacredness of human life." (President Ronald Reagan)

"I know what I'm about to say will be very controversial, but I also believe that God's greatest gift is human life and that we have a sacred duty to protect the innocent human life of an unborn child." (President Ronald Reagan)

"I praise you because I am fearfully and wonderfully made; your works are wonderful, I know them full well." (NIV Psalm 139:14)

"For you created my inmost being; you knit me together in my mother's womb." (NIV Psalm 139:13)

"Before I formed you in the womb, I knew you, before you were born I set you apart; I appointed you as a prophet to the nations." (NIV Jeremiah 1:5)

"Can a mother forget the baby at her breast and have no compassion on the child she had born? Though she may forget, I will not forget you!" (NIV Isaiah 49:15)

Janet R. Chipps

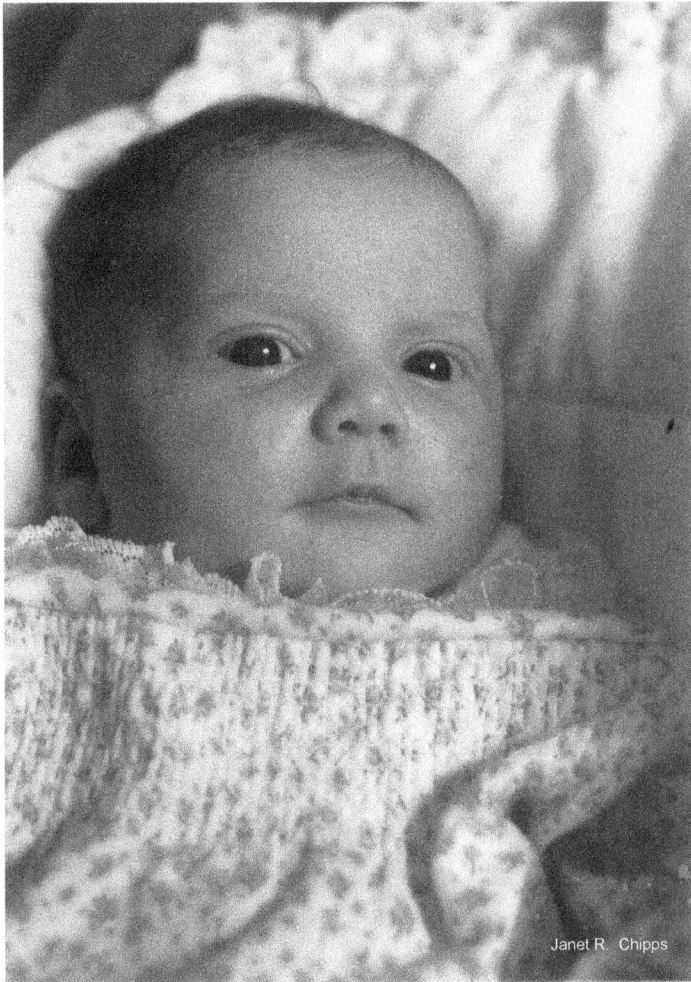

Janet R. Chipps

Chapter 3   War on Drugs

Drugs and Violence

I grew up in the sixties, as the hippie generation emerged into American culture. Millions of youth rallied to the call of love, peace and brotherhood, because the theme of this movement resonated in the hearts and minds of America's youth, namely, self expression, searching for purpose in life, and meaning for their existence. This became the embodiment of utter disdain and dissatisfaction with main stream ideology and the status-quo in society.

Rebellion against the establishment, and seeking their identity in eastern cults, socialist politics, free expression and drug use became central to their cause. In the climax of this movement, we witnessed many famous rock stars, such as Jimmie Hendrix, Janis Joplin and many others die from drug overdoses, while the bliss life on communes, such as Woodstock, collapsed into old memories.

Like many of that generation, the déjà vu, groovy, radical movement, passed away. Survivors of this era, many now who are embracing socialism, extreme liberal philosophy and secular humanism, are 60 to 70 year olds. Some grew out of it. Others entered politics and sought higher academia, and are now professors in our universities. I often wonder if these hippie kids were searching for God and didn't know how to find him. Yet, He is not far from any of us. The real message of love, peace, and brotherhood are offered to us in the gospel in biblical context.

Unlike the hippie generation of the 60's, the 70's and 80's brought a new surge of the counterculture to our youth. Many aspiring to neo-Nazism, punk rock, rap, street gang affiliation and many more lethal drugs were ushered in. No more love, peace, or brotherhood in the neighborhood. With a new boldness, the effects in the rising crime wave and drug abuse would now soar at an alarming rate. Children in single parent families, divorce, abortion, violent crime, high school drop outs, and illiteracy are rampant, statistically sky rocketing. This results in a general sense of ignorance, immorality and lawlessness now seen in epidemic proportions, not just in urban cities, but now in small rural communities throughout America.

From the early 90's to 2016, our country faces a major crisis. Chronic diseases that were non-existent prior to 1965 are now prevalent. To date there are presently 4 million people infected with hepatitis C and 1.2 million infected with HIV-Aids. One in eight are not even aware of being infected. I know this is alarming, and it should be! It is spinning out of control. Many of these infections are contracted through drug use and sexually communicative behavior.

President Ronald Reagan and Nancy Reagan

Here's what President Ronald Reagan and First Lady Nancy Reagan said over 30 years ago:

Address to the nation on the campaign against Drug Abuse, September 14, 1986

President Reagan: Good morning. Usually I talk with you from my office in the West Wing of the White House, but tonight there's something special to talk about, and I've asked someone very special to join me. Nancy and I are here in the West Hall of the White House, and around us are the rooms in which we live. It's the home you've provided for us, of which we merely have temporary custody.

Nancy's joining me because the message this evening is not my message, but ours. And we speak to you not simply as fellow citizens but as fellow parents and grandparents and as concerned neighbors. It's back-to-school time for America's children. And while drug and alcohol abuse cuts across all generations, it's especially damaging to the young people on whom our future depends. So tonight, from our family to yours, from our home to yours, thank you for joining us.

America has accomplished so much in these last few years, whether it's been rebuilding our economy or serving the cause of freedom in the world. What we've been able to achieve has been done with your help—with us working together as a nation united. Now, we need your support again. Drugs are menacing our society. They're threatening our values and undercutting our institutions. They're killing our children.

From the beginning of our administration, we've taken strong steps to do something about this horror. Tonight I can report to you that we've made much progress. Thirty-seven Federal agencies are working together in a vigorous national effort, and by next year out spending for drug law enforcement will have more than tripled from its 1981 levels. We have increased seizures of illegal drugs. Shortages of marijuana are now being reported. Last year alone over 10,000 drug criminals were convicted and nearly $250 million of their assets were seized by the DEA, the Drug Enforcement Administration.

And in the most important area, individual use, we see progress. In 4 years the number of high school seniors using marijuana on a daily basis has dropped from 1 in 14 to 1 in 20. The U.S. military has cut the use of illegal drugs among its personnel by 67 percent since 1980. These are a measure of our commitment and emerging signs that we can defeat this enemy. But we still have much to do. Despite our best efforts, illegal cocaine is coming into our country at alarming levels and 4 to 5 million people regularly use it. Five hundred thousand Americans are hooked on heroin. One in twelve persons smokes marijuana regularly. Regular drug use is even higher among the age group 18 to 25…most likely just entering the workforce. Today there's a new epidemic: crack cocaine, otherwise known as crack. It is an explosively destructive and awful lethal substance which is crushing it users. It is an uncontrolled fire.

And drug abuse is not a so-called victim-less crime. Everyone's safety is at stake when drugs and excessive alcohol are used by people on highways or by those transporting our citizens or operating industrial equipment. Drug abuse costs you and your fellow Americans at least $60 billion a year.

From the early days of our administration, Nancy has been intensely involved in the effort to fight drug abuse. She has since traveled over 100,000 miles to 55 cities in 28 states and 6 foreign countries to fight school-age drug and alcohol abuse. She's given dozens of speeches and scores of interviews and has participated in 24 special radio and TV tapings to create greater awareness of this crisis. Her personal observations and efforts have given her such dramatic insights that I wanted her to share them with you this evening.

Nancy Reagan: Thank you. As a mother I've always thought of September as a special month, a time when we bundled out children to school, to the warmth of an environment in which they could fulfill the promise and hope in those restless minds. But so much has happened over these last years, so much to shake the foundations of all that we know and all that we believe in. Today there's a drug and alcohol abuse epidemic in this country, and no one is safe from it—not you, not me, and certainly not our children, because this epidemic has their names written on it. Many of you may be thinking: "'Well, drugs don't concern me.'" But it does concern you. It concerns us all because of the way it tears at our lives and because it's aimed at destroying the brightness and life of the sons and daughters of the United States.

For five years I have been traveling across the country—learning and listening. And one of the most hopeful signs I've seen is the building of an essential, new awareness of how terrible and threatening drug abuse is to our society. This was one of the main purposes when I started, so of course it makes me happy that that's been accomplished. But each time I meet with someone new or receive another letter from a troubled person on drugs, I yearn to find a way to help share the message that cries out from them. As a parent, I'm especially concerned about what drugs are doing to young mothers and their new born children. Listen to this new account from a hospital in Florida of a child born to a mother with a cocaine habit: "'Nearby, a baby named Paul lies motionless in an incubator, feeding tubes riddling his tiny body. He needs a respirator to breathe and a daily spinal tap to relieve fluid buildup on his brain. Only 1 month old, he's already suffered 2 strokes.'"

Now you can see why drug abuse concerns every one of us—all the American family. Drugs steal away so much. They take and take, until finally every time a drug goes into a child, something else is forced out—like love and hope and trust and confidence. Drugs take away the dream from every child's heart and replaces it with a nightmare, and it's time we in America stand up and replace these dreams. Each of us has to put our principles and consciences on the line, whether in social settings or in the workplace, to set forth solid standards and stick to them. There's no moral middle ground. Indifference is not an option. We want you to help us create an outspoken intolerance for drug use. For the sake of our children, I implore each of you to be unyielding and inflexible in your opposition to drugs.

Our young people are helping us lead the way. Not long ago, in Oakland, California, I was asked by a group of children what to do it they were offered drugs, and I answered, "'Just say no.'" Soon after that, those children in Oakland formed a Just Say No club, and now there are over 10,000 such clubs all over the country. Well, their participation and their courage in saying no needs our encouragement. We can help by using every opportunity to force the issue of not using drugs to the point of making others uncomfortable, even if it means making ourselves unpopular.

Our job is never easy because drug criminals are ingenious. They work everyday to plot a new and better way to steal our children's lives, just as they've done by developing this new drug, crack. For every door that we close, they open a new door to death. They prosper on our unwillingness to act. So, we must be smarter and stronger and tougher than they are. It's up to us to change attitudes and just simply dry up their markets.

And finally, to you people watching or listening, I have a very personal message for you: There's a big, wonderful world out there for you. It belongs to you. It's exciting and stimulating and rewarding. Don't cheat yourselves out of this promise. Our country needs you, but it needs you to be clear-eyed and clear-minded. I recently read a teenager's story. She's now determined to stay clean but was once strung out on several drugs. What she remembered most clearly about her recovery was that during the time she was on drugs everything appeared to her in shades of black and gray and after her treatment she was able to see colors again.

So, to my young friends out there: Life can be great, but not when you can't see it. So, open your eyes to life: to see it in the vivid colors that God gave us as a precious gift to his children, to enjoy life to the fullest, and to make it count. Say yes to your life. And when it comes to drugs and alcohol just say no.

President Reagan: I think we can see why Nancy has been such a positive influence on all that we're trying to do. The job ahead of is very clear. Nancy's personal crusade, like that of so many other wonderful individuals, should become our national crusade. It must include a combination of government and private efforts which complement one another. Last month I announced six initiatives which we believe will do just that.

First, we seek a drug-free workplace at all levels of government and in the private sector. Second, we'll work toward drug-free schools. Third, we want to ensure that the public is protected and that treatment is available to substance abusers and the chemically dependent. Our fourth goal is to expand international cooperation while treating drug trafficking as a threat to our national security. In October I will be meeting with key U.S. Ambassadors to discuss what can be done to support our friends abroad. Fifth, we must move to strengthen law enforcement activities such as those initiated by Vice President Bush and Attorney General Meese. And finally, we seek to expand public awareness and prevention.

In order to further implement these six goals, I will announce tomorrow a series of new proposals for a drug-free America. Taken as a whole, these proposals will toughen our laws against drug criminals, encourage more research and treatment, and ensure that illegal drugs will not be tolerated in our schools or in our workplaces. Together with our ongoing efforts, these proposals will bring the Federal commitment to fighting drugs to $3 billion. As much financing as we commit, however, we would be fooling ourselves if we thought that massive new amounts of money alone will provide the solution. Let us not forget that in America people solve problems and no national crusade has ever succeeded without human investment. Winning the crusade against drugs will not be achieved by just throwing money at the problem. Your government will continue to act aggressively, but nothing would be more effective than for Americans simply to quit using illegal drugs. We seek to create a massive change in national attitudes which ultimately will separate the drugs from the customer, to take the user away from the supply. I believe, quite simply, that we can help them quit, and that's where you come in.

My generation will remember how America swung into action when we were attacked in World War II. The war was not just fought by the fellows flying the planes or driving the tanks. It was fought at home by a mobilized nation—men and women alike—building planes and ships, clothing sailors and soldiers, feeding marines and airmen; and it was fought by children planting victory gardens and collecting cans. Well, now we're in another war for our freedom, and it's time for all of us to pull together again. So, for example, if your friend or neighbor or a family member has a drug or alcohol problem, don't turn the other way. Go to his help or to hers. Get others involved with you—clubs, service groups, and community organizations—help provide support and strength. And, of course, many of you've been cured through treatment and self-help. Well, you're the combat veterans, and you have a critical role to play. You can help others by telling your story and providing a willing hand to those in need. Being friends to others is the best way of being friends to ourselves. It's time, as Nancy said, for America to "'Just say no'" to drugs.

Those of you in union halls and workplaces everywhere: Please make this challenge a part of your job every day. Help us preserve the health and dignity of all workers. To business large and small: We need the creativity of your enterprise applied directly to this national problem. Help us. And those of you who are educators: Your wisdom and leadership are indispensable to this cause. From the pulpits of this spirit-filled land: We would welcome your reassuring message of redemption and forgiveness and of helping one another. On the athletic fields: You men and women are among the most beloved citizens of our country. A child's eyes filled with your heroic achievements. Few can give youngsters something as special and strong to look up to as you. Please don't let them down.

And this camera in front of us: It's a reminder that in Nancy's and my former profession and in the newsrooms and production rooms of our media centers—you have a special opportunity with your enormous influence to send alarm signals across the

Nation. To our friends in foreign countries: We know many of you are involved in this battle with us. We need your success as well as ours. When we all come together, united, striving for this cause, then those who are killing America and terrorizing it with slow but sure chemical destruction will see that they are up against the mightiest force for good that we know. Then they will not have dark alleyways to hide in.

In this crusade, let us not forget who we are. Drug abuse is a repudiation of everything America is. The destructiveness and human wreckage mock our heritage. Think for a moment how special it is to be an American. Can we doubt that only a divine providence placed this land, this island of freedom, here as a refuge for all those people of the world who yearn to be free?

The revolution out of which our liberty was conceived signaled an historical call to an entire world seeking hope. Each new arrival of immigrants rode the crest of that hope. They came, millions seeking a safe harbor from the oppression of cruel regimes. They came, to escape starvation and disease. They came, those surviving the Holocaust and the Soviet gulags. They came, the boat people, chancing death for even a glimmer of hope that they could have a new life. They all came to taste the air redolent and rich with the freedom that is ours. What an insult it will be to what we are and whence we came if we do not rise up together in defiance against this cancer of drugs.

And there's one more thing. The freedom that so many seek in our land has not been preserved without a price. Nancy and I shared that remembrance two years ago at the Normandy American Cemetery in France. In the still of that June afternoon, we walked together among the soldiers of freedom, past the hundreds of white markers which are monuments to courage and memorials to sacrifice. Too many of these and other such graves are the final resting places of teenagers who became men in the roar of battle.

Look what they gave to us who live. Never would they see another sunlit day glistening off a lake or river back home or miles of corn pushing up against the open sky of our plains. The pristine air of our mountains and the driving energy of our cities are theirs no more. Nor would they ever again be a son to their parents or a father to their own children. They did this for you, for me, for a new generation to carry our democratic experiment proudly forward. Well, that's something I think we're obliged to honor, because what they did for us means that we owe as a simple act of civic stewardship to use our freedom wisely for the common good.

As we mobilize for this national crusade, I'm mindful that drugs are a constant temptation for millions. Please remember this when your courage is tested: you are Americans. You're the product of the freest society mankind has ever known. No one, ever, has the right to destroy your dreams and shatter your life.

Right down the end of this hall is the Lincoln Bedroom. But in the Civil War that room was the one President Lincoln used as his office. Memory fills that room, and more than anything that memory drives us to see vividly what President Lincoln sought to save. Above all, it is that America must stand for something and that our heritage lets us stand with a strength of character made more steely be each layer of challenge pressed upon the nation. We Americans have never been morally neutral against any form of tyranny. Tonight we're asking no more than that we honor what we have been and what we are by standing together.

Mrs. Reagan: Now we go on to the next stop: making a final commitment not to tolerate drugs by anyone, anytime, anyplace. So won't you join us in this great, new, national crusade?

President Reagan: God bless you, and good night.

Note: The President spoke at 8pm from the Residence of the White House. The address was broadcast live on nationwide radio and television.

This speech was made 32 years ago. Since that time the drug epidemic has surged to startling proportions. New and more lethal drugs are now common, inexpensive and available, such as crystal meth. This drug was used by Nazis in World War II and is now the drug of choice throughout America. The death toll over the past 30 years has exceeded all casualties of all the wars combined, and there is no sign of this trend slowing down. If this plague is not checked, many more people will die, or become like zombies and misfits drifting through the streets. It will reap havoc and spark anarchy and lawless crime in

ways we never could think imaginable. This problem
has been quietly ignored for far too long. Much must
be done, and soon, if there is any hope of ending this
nightmare in America.

A crew member aboard the Coast Guard Cutter Legare stacks
a bale of cocaine during a contraband offload at Coast Guard
Base Miami Beach, Fla., Sept. 4, 2014. The offload is the result
of two successful drug interdictions in the Caribbean Sea.

In the summer of 2012, my wife and I experienced one of the most devastating tragedies that parents can ever face. We lost two children to drug, violent-related death's. Our daughter, 29 year old Seva, and our 25 year old son, Matthew, were killed violently as a result of this plague in our culture. Drug related crime is so pervasive in American society, that very few families are insulated from its far reaching effects. Although we as a family have experienced a great loss, you cannot bring your loved ones back once they are gone. I hope and wish no other parent would ever have to go through this experience.

My wife and I both understand one thing: "The Lord giveth, and the Lord taketh away. Blessed be the name of the Lord." He has been our rock, and our anchor, through all of the pain. We have learned a lot since then, pertaining to just how big a problem the drug epidemic in America has become, and the violence that's attributed directly as a result. As Parents, I truly hope you never have to bury your children. I am convinced, and of the conviction, that if we as a nation do not get the drugs and drug dealers off the streets of America, we will witness the total collapse of the American culture. The drugs that are killing our kids are extremely dangerous. Crystal methamphetamines, crack cocaine and heroin are common and accessible in virtually every part of the country. It must be stopped! We can do what is necessary to get it stopped. Will we?

MAY THE LORD BLESS AND KEEP
YOU, MAY HIS FACE SHINE UPON
YOU AND GIVE YOU PEACE. MAY HE
BE GRACIOUS TO YOU ALL OF YOUR
DAYS. 8-10-1982 3-9-2012
  HEPHZIVAH LEE CHIPPS

Janet R. Chipps

Matthew James Chipps 6-20-1986
passed away 6-4-2012

Janet R. Chipps

...May you find a special place in His kingdom...

Chapter 4
National Security and U.S. Borders

I was born on the West Coast in 1960. Growing up I remember asking my mother, "Hey, mom, who are all those guys sitting on the side of the over pass, and why are they there?" There were dozens; all the time, every day. She told me they were Mexican immigrants looking for work. When I got older, I got in to the construction industry and worked and lived in Colorado and Texas for a period of over 30 years. In both states, at that time, there were many illegal aliens in the construction industry. This was in the early 80's. At first, many of the illegal immigrants worked as laborers for many people and businesses. As time went on, I began to notice businesses springing up everywhere, owned and operated by these illegal laborers.

In the mid 80's, the country fell into a recession, and the building industry was seriously affected by the poor economy. I found that my competition in business was with illegal Mexican nationals who were operating their own businesses. I was licensed, bonded and insured. I advertised and paid taxes. This is a real problem in America.

We have, in estimates that vary between 12-15 million, undocumented and illegal aliens here in the United States. They do not pay federal taxes because they do not have a social security number or card. I have worked very hard my whole life in the construction industry-- over 40 years. As a middle income family man, with a small business, my experience with illegal populations working here in the U.S.A., has not proved to be lucrative. The illegal laborers work for cash and do not report their income. This is a well known fact, unless you live in a bubble or teach at a university, and have had no association with reality, in the American workforce.

The reality of the economic effects is far reaching. At age 52, I had an injury and went to the emergency room at Citizen's Hospital in Victoria, Texas. The surgeon on call was so overwhelmed with treating illegal immigrants that I could not be seen for over 8 hours—with a compound break on my ankle. I have discovered since then, that hospitals across America are experiencing similar situations. These hospitals are required to provide services to the entire population of illegal immigrants regardless of their inability to pay. I received a bill for over $20,000. As U.S. citizens, the cost to American tax payers for these and other free government services, provided to the illegal population, is estimated in the hundreds of billions of dollars.

In doing some research, I was able to verify some very interesting facts. If an American enters Mexico and attempts to work, he or she will be fined, jailed and deported immediately, nine out of ten times. You cannot purchase land in Mexico if you are not a citizen there. Americans lease land but cannot own it. U.S. law states that it is a felony to enter the United States illegally.

Our country has become tolerant to the extent of carelessly endangering American interests and lives. We fail to enforce the laws of our constitution, and promote the notion that there are no borders.

This is an injustice and is unfair to all American citizens. The drug trafficking and human trafficking coming in from Mexico is so out of control, and such an immense and monumental problem, most people cannot begin to understand or grasp its negative impact on the USA.

Mexican drug cartels and gangs have purchased ranches, homes and businesses here in America on a large scale. Hundreds of billions of dollars in the illegal drug trade annually occurs and the establishment of violent Mexican gangs have set up shop in most cities across our country. Like radical Islamic terrorism, it is equally as dangerous, and is considered, and should be, a serious national security threat to our nation. Although it appears to be domestic in nature, the ramifications are reaping a deadly consequence.

Tens of thousands of our youth fall prey to the plague of drugs entering this country every day from Mexico. The annual death toll, as a result of this fact, is like unto the casualties of war. In fact, all the wars America has fought combined, do not exceed the death toll due to drugs and its associated violence over the past 30 years. If it's not a war, it should be. Over 1.5 million deaths have occurred directly as a result of this problem. We need to secure our borders and get staunchly tough in the war on drugs.

The issues concerning national security on the border are widespread. The 13 individual terrorists from Saudi Arabia who participated in the 9-11 attacks entered the US through Mexico. If young children can walk across on a day to day basis it leads one to reason that certainly a trained terrorist can do the same. The incidents involving repeat convicted felons of Mexican national descent are far too numerous to list in this book. We can honestly say that violent offenders commit many horrific crimes, including assault, robbery, rape and murder and are not prosecuted, but often released. I know this to be true personally, because I lived in the states where these crimes were committed and I can affirm to you, in this written statement, that it is true.

Securing the border is no longer an option but a mandate of necessity; to do otherwise will prove disastrous. I do believe that many of the immigrants from Mexico have good intentions and dream of freedom from the oppressive and violent culture they experience in Mexico. These folks I would encourage and welcome to America, as long as they enter legally and civilly, just like our forefathers did before us.

"A nation that cannot control its borders is not a nation." (President Ronald Reagan)

"In the first place, we should insist that if the immigrant who comes here in good faith becomes an American and assimilates himself to us, he shall be treated on an exact equality with everyone else. It is an outrage to discriminate against any man, because of creed, birthplace or origin, but this is predicated upon the person becoming in every facet an American. There can be no divided allegiance here. Any man who says he is an American, but something else also, isn't an American at all. We have room for but one flag; we have room for but one language here, and that is the English language; we have

room for but one sole loyalty and that is loyalty to the American people." (President Theodore Roosevelt)

"The immigrant is not Americanized unless his interest and affections have become deeply rooted here, and we properly demand of the immigrant even more than this. He must be brought into complete harmony with our ideas and aspirations and cooperate with us for their attainment. Only when this has been done will he posses the national consciousness of an American."
(Ann Coulter, conservative commentator)

On the issue of immigration, it appears that there may be a vested interest on behalf of the liberal left. Their pretense of compassion for displaced people from abroad, and advocating a mass migration to our country, without thought of the cost, both in dollars and potential threat of terroristic results, is incomprehensible, while they pledge to continue in this very expensive and dangerous pattern of importing thousands, even millions, of immigrants into our country. There appears to be a large consensus against this action within our country's population.

America is in debt trillions of dollars. Our culture and our economy are suffering dramatically, and yet we fail to consider "the straws on the camel's back". How many straws will liberal leftist pile on the backs of Americans until the back will utterly break! If these folks on the left are wanting to acquire and import votes in exchange for entitlements to assure their future quest of absolute despotism, maybe they should come up with an idea that will actually help Americans to secure the economy and stabilize civility and bring positive, prosperous and noble ideas to the table.

Basic common sense and reason is virtually rare and close to non-existent in proposals of the radical left wing liberal party. No wonder they lost so woefully in the 2016 elections. Thank God America is waking up. We must be sober, wise and cautious when considering the mass importation of refugees from regions that propagate, teach, and encourage acts of terrorism against American citizens. You cannot vet idealism from people who have been steeped in the notion of killing Americans as a good cause. Many radical Islamic groups promote this doctrine of belief. I really do believe they would better acclimate in regions that they are familiar with and find common to their ideologies. Other countries in the middle east will be much better suited for this purpose, and their assimilation to those cultures would be much easier and cost effective.

Let's put the brakes on here and get control of ourselves before the train goes off the tracks. Have we learned from Europe any lessons at all? They experience these random attacks from radical Islamic extremists on a day to day basis. To be honest, I cannot, in the furthest reaches of my imagination, believe that this is even being considered as a project from the left. These folks come up with the craziest ideas I have ever heard of. Regression should be in their new title—Radical Regressive Left Wing Liberals for America's Demise. That sounds like a great new slogan for this brazen bunch. Are not these the same liberals, the one's proposing a lunar colony on mars? Let's get 'em one step closer to their goal and do like the British did, put 'em on an island they can call their own; all of them; as soon as possible and pay for it until they grow up and can fend for themselves!

I have to apologize for my attitude, but the absurdity and consistent incomprehension displayed on the left is ludicrous and intangible to the common man. I would donate 5% of my income if these folks would voluntarily expel themselves from our great union of these United States; if they promise not to return until they come to their senses and are fully rehabilitated.

"If we're so cruel to minorities, why do they keep coming here; why aren't they sneaking across the Mexican border to make their way to the Taliban?" (Ann Coulter, conservative commentator)

"I think Donald Trump taps into an anger that I hear every day. People are angry that a common sense thing like securing the border or ending sanctuary cities is something extreme. It's not extreme, it's common sense. We need to secure the border." (Carly Fiorina)

"Last year there were roughly 540,000 people detained coming across the border illegally. 45,000 of them came from countries other than Mexico, demonstrating the fact that Mexico itself now is the pathway into the United States for people all around the world, and we don't know what their intentions are." (Senator John Cornyn)

"If Israel sees weapons, or illegal groups moving toward its border it acts, as does every other nation in the entire world." (Richard Engel)

"I am certain that I speak on behalf of my entire nation when I say: Sept. 11 we are all Americans–in grief, as in defiance." (Benjamin Netanyahu, Prime Minister of Israel)

I am going to create a new special deportation task force, focused on identifying and removing quickly the most dangerous criminal illegal immigrants in America. Our enforcement priorities will include removing criminals, gang members, security threats, visa over stays, and public charges, that is, those relying on public welfare or straining the safety net. For those here today illegally who are seeking legal status, they will have one route and only one route: to return home and apply for re-entry. When we have accomplished all of our enforcement goals and truly ended illegal immigration for good, including the construction of a great wall, and the establishment of our new lawful immigration system, then and only then will we be in a position to consider the

President Donald J. Trump

appropriate disposition of those who remain. Not everyone who seeks to join our country will be able to successfully assimilate. It is our right as a sovereign nation to choose immigrants that we think are likeliest to thrive and flourish here. While there are many illegal immigrants in our country who are good people, this doesn't change the fact that most illegal immigrants are lower skilled workers with less education who compete directly against vulnerable American workers. Anyone who illegally crosses will be detained until they are removed and go back to the country from which they came. And they will be brought great distances. We are not dropping them right across. The time has come for a new immigration commission to develop a new set of reforms to our legal immigration system in order to achieve the following goals: to keep immigration levels measured by population within historical norms; to select immigrants based on their likelihood of success in the U.S., and their ability to be financially self sufficient." (President Donald Trump)

Chapter 5
Economic Growth, Jobs and Debt

The basis for any economic plan being successful is stimulated by the free market of capitalism working without the heavy restraints and regulations imposed by the federal government in order for free enterprise to flourish and grow. In addition, incentives are an inert ingredient in kick starting a stale and sluggish economy.

According to reliable sources, the Obama administration, in the prior eight years, yielded more debt than all the prior administrations combined.
This is unprecedented in American history. This fact is true: An additional 53 million American families are on welfare, and the national debt is at its record highest. Hundreds of billions of tax payer dollars have been given to countries like Iran, who themselves claim to be a sworn enemy. Combine all the entitlement programs added to this, it's no wonder why, during the Obama administration, the only thing that got done well was the endless printing of money, and out-of-control spending.

President Trump, a successful businessman and loyal American is the best thing that the U.S. could possibly hope for since Ronald Reagan. If Trump truly implements the policies he has promised, there's no reason why the U.S. economy will not fully recover and prosperity again can flourish throughout the country and world wide. I supported Donald Trump from the beginning because I believe he is honest, sober-minded and sees America for what it is now and what it can potentially become in the future.

He is not a perfect man, but he is the perfect man for the job.

Congratulations sir, on your recent win to the White House. I can honestly say, for the first time in over a decade, that I am encouraged and refreshed by our victory as Americans. If you did not support Donald Trump in the election, I truly believe you will when you see our country back up on its feet and running again like America should. I am in agreement with President Trump on most of the issues he campaigned on, and will support him in prayer as we all should. Scripture implores us to pray for our leaders and this man is a leader. If given the chance, we can again be proud of America and assist in making America great again.

I believe that common sense and clear insight to the approach to our country's struggles are at the core of our new president's vision and concerns. For such a time as this in history, we need good judgment and wise and vigilant leadership at the helm of the ship, so we can sail again on the voyage to the future, only to look back and draw encouragement from those who went before us. Inspired by their courage, and determination to hold the standard high, we now press on in the fight to keep America free and strong. With providence dispensed from heaven and the angels of the Almighty God at our Creator's beckoning, we can again hope for prosperity and be steadfast in our desire to see America move forward with clear objectives and realistic goals.

I am not an expert on economics, but I do know the difference between stagnant and robust. Every honest person in America knows beyond a shadow of a doubt that we have had an extremely stagnant economy. In the past eight years inflation has soared, wages are frozen, earnings and net growth are at their lowest in history. It is no wonder so many are receiving subsistence and barely surviving. This isn't normal. Most people want to work hard and to do well; they just need opportunity.

According to recent statistics, there are now far more U.S. manufacturing jobs shipped to Mexico and overseas, employing foreigners, than there are U.S. manufacturing jobs employing American workers.

American corporations have moved abroad, where they could acquire cheap labor and essential components in order to make higher profits importing finished products back into the U.S. I understand that legal policies and labor unions prompted this action. Needless regulations and higher taxes imposed by the left also contributed to the larger corporations fleeing this country. Now for the first time in over 25 years, we have a president who understands this and is willing to actually do something about it.

Very bad trade deals, like NAFTA, made by President Bill Clinton had catastrophic effects causing a near collapse of the U.S. economy. President Trump has taken initiative in these issues of policy. His plan to impose penalties via higher tax rates to U.S. companies abroad importing their goods back into the U.S. is an excellent plan. It's very reasonable and a fair way to deal with this problem.

Energy is a key strategy and component of the very infrastructure of America. It is also an issue of national security. The U.S. has massive oil and gas resources throughout the country, but especially in Alaska. Virtually untapped, Alaska, according to experts, has oil and gas resources capable of sustaining a supply to the U.S. for, in some estimates, over two hundred years.

I live in Alaska. The economy here has been in a serious recession since President Obama was elected. On the North Slope of Alaska and in the Arctic, is a vast supply of oil and gas. A large majority of the Alaskan population welcomes the idea of drilling for oil and gas. Congressman Young and Senator Sullivan are both proponents of this plan here in Alaska.

Alaska is a huge state. Most of the region where oil and gas drilling will occur is uninhabited, there are no roads and the environment here will not be negatively impacted if done in a safe manner. If as a nation, we continue to rely on the middle east and do not prepare for energy independence, those supplies in Saudi Arabia will be sorely depleted and will dwindle at a rapid rate.

We will have a shortage one day soon, capable of halting commerce and transportation as we know it. It's a very real problem. The instability in the Middle East and OPEC, declaring shortages in this commodity, must lead us to conclude that oil, gas and coal production in Alaska is an absolute necessity and high priority for America's economy and national security.

Clearly, if nothing else teaches us a lesson, we can learn from our debt. The U.S. national debt will never be removed until we, as a nation, learn a very basic rule in economics. President Trump said it best: "Jobs, jobs, jobs. *All hard work brings a reward.*" (Proverbs 14:23)

This age-old concept really works. Generating income through commerce and collective taxes on that commerce, equals a robust economy and rewards us, if, as good stewards of the wealth we attain, we can address the debt. In a reliable and sustainable economy, when everyone is working, prosperity will ensue and we can actually get out of debt.

The problem is twofold. Liberal politicians do not believe in a work ethic, and they spend America's tax dollars, borrowing from our children and grand children, just so they can give it to our enemies in Iran, who would like to blow America and Israel off the map. I don't mean to sound factious. This is not Einstein's Quantum Physics; this is economics101. If President Trump seems old fashioned, we really need some old fashioned common sense. No wonder he gets so frustrated with ignorant people who pretend to tell the truth. Our forefathers were also old fashioned and they founded the greatest country in the world. Let's learn from them.

"To contract new debts is not the way to pay old ones." (President George Washington)

President Benjamin Harrison

President Grover Cleveland

President Calvin Coolidge

"It is the responsibility of the citizen to support their government. It is not the responsibility of the government to support its citizens."
(President Grover Cleveland)

"We Americans have no commission from God to police the world." (President Benjamin Harrison) (Author's Comment: This is a very expensive and a risky endeavor)

"A government which has taxes on the people not required by urgent public necessity and serving public policy is not a protector of liberty, but an instrument of tyranny." (President Calvin Coolidge)

"When a business or an individual spends more than it makes, it goes bankrupt. When government does it, it sends you the bill and when government does it for 40 years, the bill comes in two ways: higher taxes and inflation."
(President Ronald Reagan)

"We in government should learn to look at our country with the eyes of entrepreneurs, seeing the possibilities where others see only problems."
(President Ronald Reagan)

"No nation has ever taxed itself into financial prosperity." (Rush Limbaugh, commentator)

"The United States is a giant island of freedom, achievement, wealth, and prosperity in a world hostile to our values."
(Phyllis Schlafly, political activist and author.)

"The power to tax involves the power to destroy." (John Marshall, U.S. Chief Justice, Supreme Court)

"And to preserve their independence, we must not let our rulers load us with perpetual debt."
(President Thomas Jefferson)

President Thomas Jefferson

Chapter 6
Rebuilding U.S. Military Infrastructure

Having a strong military in the age of uncertainty is paramount. High tech weaponry capabilities developed by our enemies pose a deadly threat to America's ability to defend itself. I believe in a defensive strategy and posture, rather than an offensive position.

I'm not implying that certain actions should not be taken when America's safety and security are at risk. The problems that exist in today's world require us as Americans to be ready and capable of responding to aggression in a timely and effective manner, without getting American soldiers killed. The advances in high tech weaponry address these concerns. We have to maintain the highest standard of readiness and efficiency with the ability to be mobile and swift in the event of impending attacks.

The nature of fighting has changed significantly as technology advances at a very rapid rate. Our equipment is aged, so our readiness is compromised, no matter how vigilant we remain. The U.S. military was reduced considerably by the Clinton administration during the 90's. It has suffered budget cuts during eight years of Obama. The liberal view of "poorer and weaker" for the U.S. military is a slogan I hope is gone forever. We do not want to use the U.S. military's strength and ability unless no other option is available. If we are forced to engage our enemy, we had better be ready.

"To be prepared for war is one of the most effectual means of preserving peace."
(President George Washington)

"Our debt to the heroic men and valiant women in the service of our country can never be repaid.
They have earned our undying gratitude. America with never forget their sacrifices."
(President Harry Truman)

Photo: Library of Congress

President Harry Truman

"A truly successful army is one that, because of its strength and ability and dedication, will not be called on to fight, for no one will dare to provoke it." (President Ronald Reagan)

"An America that is militarily and economically strong is not enough. The world must see an America that is morally strong with a creed and a vision. This is what has led us to dare and achieve. For us, values count." (President Ronald Reagan)

"We've been blessed with the opportunity to stand for something for liberty and freedom and fairness, and these are things worth fighting for; devoting our lives to." (President Ronald Reagan)

The federal government's constitutional obligation to provide an adequate military and proper infrastructure via roads, public transportation, and secure borders, is required as a mandate in the U.S. constitution. The neglect of these issues is a blatant miscarriage of the responsibilities charged to any administration. In lieu of the immense burden of financing liberal entitlement programs, these funds should be typically applied to the much needed repairs and re-bolstering of our infrastructure. Hopefully soon, our economy will experience a vibrant boost and sustained growth in order to complete the task.

President Trump has a big mess to clean up after the Obama administration's grossly managed and misappropriation of U.S. tax dollars. It will now be very expensive, due to the inadequacy of Obama's wild and careless spending spree that left the United

States in debt, more so in his eight year term than all presidents in American history combined. The reinvestment in America's military and infrastructure is vital to the budget and will now take longer and cost more due to its neglect during Obama's term. It will be challenging and will require wise consideration by law makers on just how to do this efficiently. So much money and time has been squandered by liberal politicians in their haphazard entitlement spending programs, it is no wonder why America is suffering so much.

"I pray heaven to bestow the best of blessings on this house (White House) and on all that hereafter inhabit it . May none but honest and wise men ever rule under this roof." (President John Adams)

Chapter 7
Mass Media's Greatest Cover Up

Just to ease your mind and spare you further disappointment, I want to clarify in the beginning of this chapter, one very important point. First, my view is not based on preconceived notions or opinions expressed in some conspiracy plot. The documentation required in presenting fact as truth can easily be verified (substantially) by simply using Google or any reliable resource. So it is not an opinion or a view implied in the following statements that you will ascertain, I made it my primary objective to only state facts from established, reliable and credible sources. Unlike many in the media, who consistently offer opinions, both biased and often inaccurate; you can be sure only facts will make the case to expose what many consider to be a monumental problem with journalism and news reporting.

Most people know there is a problem with the media's lack of credibility and the fact that extreme bias exists in almost all reporting, especially in the arena of politics, but it goes far beyond that. The stigma placed squarely on the mass media has become one of distrust and incompetence, displayed in the seemingly trivial issues covered on a day by day basis.

For example, in order to clearly see a pattern of thinking, news networks have established certain criteria in order to process and report a story. In the presentation of using credible resources and accurate information, reporting each story is intended to achieve a certain outcome. In other words, if they say the grass is greener on the other side of the fence, it most likely is the side of the fence they desire their viewers to be on. You say then, there must be a vested interest in their view of that side of the fence. Precisely, because in the reporter's opinion and view, the grass is always greener on the side he or she prefers.

That is where the media has spun out of control. Today, if anything happens out of the ordinary, the media sends overly aggressive reporters who strive to be the first to get the big story. Often times they fail to verify any of the facts so they can get it broadcasted first. Now that is very common and somewhat irresponsible in terms of malice. If we can promote the practice of journalism from Sean Hannity or One America News, we will all benefit because they have a real sense of personal responsibility. Their integrity and reputation are at stake. When Sean Hannity speaks, there may be 10 million viewers watching and listening.

Honesty and honor are the vital characteristics in responsible journalism. Unfortunately, most of the reporters and commentators lack these qualities. In order to get real news that is balanced, fair, unbiased and accurate, you must have a reliable source. That is one of the many reasons that I choose to watch One America News. It's the only network that strives to adhere to the principles of honest news reporting. That being said, what possible vested interest could other networks be advocating or promoting? Good question!

Did you know that it is a fact that over 95% of the reporters, journalists and commentators at ABC, NBC, CBS, CNN, and MSNBC are registered democrats with very strong and outspoken views regarding the radical left agenda? The agenda promoted by the media juggernaut is broad and far reaching. It begins with the viewpoint that mankind can solve and manage all of the problems that exist, either individually or collectively in society. This humanistic approach eliminates any need for God or the principles of traditional values many of us, as Americans, truly appreciate and adhere to. This leaves us in a vacuum of men's opinions, preferred over any absolute standard of truth, represented in the commandments of God or the gospel teachings. There is a very distinct difference, but to claim to be unbiased is simply impossible, and to remain neutral would be like comparing the creationist view to the theory of evolution. They are two very diametrically opposing views that have nothing in common.

You may say, "What does that have to do with news reporting?" Think about it for a minute. Let's talk about the issue of homosexuality. On the one side proponents argue their view about it being an individual choice for each person. On the other side God's word is explicitly clear that those who engage in such behavior are acting morally reprehensibly. This is a consistent pattern in our society today. Whether you're speaking about abortion, drugs, or who the next president should be, all of us express a viewpoint that is bias or promotes one perspective over another. This type of mindset and thinking is what's referred to as "preferential choice".

Based on men's opinion versus an absolute standard measured and established in biblical principles, it doesn't matter what the discussion is about. There exists only one truth in a matter regardless of what the question is. This is why the problems are not being solved in today's society. When the vast majority of our news media reports with a specific intended result, we are getting a humanist liberal view relating to that issue. In order to get honest, responsible, and truthfully informative news, it matters a lot where you get your information, because it will form within you a specific view based on the source from which you get it. This is what folks refer to as 'spin'.

When the humanist media spins the news, it literally means to tweak, twist or turn it, in such a way that a desired outcome of perception is achieved, based upon how the story is told. This agenda rendered news is not a new concept. It has been around a long time and is truly propaganda oriented. The very definition of the word propaganda is: "information, especially of a biased or misleading nature, used to promote or publicize a particular political cause or point of view"—synonymous with the word spin.

Propaganda oriented news was used in Nazi Germany during the rise of Hitler. It is used as a tool in Russia in order to gain support for communist regimes. This outcome based propaganda is effectively used in many countries; some through state or nation based and owned news media sources.

"By the skillful and sustained use of propaganda one can make a people see even heaven as hell or an extremely wretched life as paradise."
(Adolf Hitler)

"Let me control the media and I will turn any nation into a herd of pigs."
(Nazi propaganda minister, Joseph Goebbels)

"Make the lie big, make it simple, keep saying it, and eventually they will believe it." (Adolf Hitler)

The mass media of America has become totally secular or worldly; it is generating a world view apart from God in all of its presentation. The honor and value system of journalism is almost extinct, because those who are responsible to deliver the news have become virtually godless, aspiring to views of evolution, humanism and atheistic or agnostic beliefs. The best way to reverse this cycle is to simply boycott the major networks and demand change in the form of requiring these networks to hire qualified reporters and commentators who are capable of reporting traditional, value based, news. This form of reporting will best represent the views of the 240 million viewers in America who adhere to biblical principles.

Chapter 8
Restoring Judeo Christian Values and Virtues

America was founded as a nation over 240 years ago. During that period of time we engaged in 12 wars. We faced deadly plagues, viruses and diseases, only to discover the cures and overcome our illnesses. We have advanced in technology, from riding on horseback and sailing ships as our only form of transportation to sending men and women into space and successfully landing on the moon. Computers, television, phones and fast food are the ear mark of some accomplishments due to our ability to harness and generate electricity, and create the gas engine. All this has been done in the past 135 years.

We have much to be thankful for in all these advancements, inventions and discoveries. One thing that has not changed, and remains constant, the most integral, steady and necessary component, is our ever present help in the time of need. God's faithfulness, is the source of a single cause, not something that a man has done, but something that no man can ever do. The word history is derived and defined as "the story authored by the Creator of heaven and earth." It's true. In all the history of mankind, you can see the providential and hidden hand of Almighty God, raising up kingdoms and conquering civilizations through the mighty acts of God.

God's righteousness reigns down from heaven upon mankind, expressing his love for us as a father to his children. It began thousands of years ago in a garden with Adam and Eve, later to the Hebrew nation and then through the gospel to the entire world. The bible is the oldest script text ever discovered in modern time. Nearly 5000 years of history are found between its covers, and though it is ancient, it remains the bestselling book ever written or published.

Many nations, notably powerful, are written about in its pages, recorded for us to remember and, though many nations have been conquered, only a few remain. America is one of those nations in whom God has shed his grace and with that privilege comes an obligation inherent to all who acknowledge this fact. The Ten Commandments are not just for the Jews, nor is the story of Joseph, Mary and Jesus just for the Gentiles. An estimated 2.5 billion people today are comprised of both Jews and Christians worldwide.

Read and listen to what famous people have said about our great country and remember to encourage others who share in our great heritage. We have been given and entrusted with much.

"It is impossible to govern a nation without God and the bible." (President George Washington)

President George Washington

President John Adams

"Statesmen, my dear Sir, may plan and speculate for Liberty, but it is Religion and Morality alone, which can establish the Principles upon which Freedom can securely stand. The only foundation of a free Constitution is pure Virtue, and if this cannot be inspired into our People in a greater Measure than they have it now. They may change their Rulers and the forms of Government, but they will not obtain a lasting Liberty. They will only exchange tyrants and Tyrannies." (John Adams)

"May our country be always successful, but whether successful or otherwise, always right."
(President John Quincy Adams)

"Posterity—you will never know how much it has cost my generation to preserve your freedom. I hope you will make good use of it."
(President John Quincy Adams)

President John Quincy Adams

"Without God, there is no virtue, because there's no prompting of the conscience. Without God, we're mired in the material, that flat world that tells us only what the senses perceive. Without God, there is a coarsening of the society, and without God, democracy will not, and cannot, long endure. If we ever forget that we are one nation under God, then we will be a nation gone under." (President Ronald Reagan)

"(Our goal) is to help revive American traditional values: faith, family, neighborhood, work and freedom. Government has no business enforcing these values, but neither must it seek, as it did in the recent past, to suppress or replace them. That only robbed us of our tiller and set us adrift."
(President Ronald Reagan)

"Helping to restore these values will bring new strength, direction and dignity to our lives and to the life of our nation. It's on these values that we'll best build our future." (President Ronald Reagan)

"Fellow Americans, our duty is before us tonight. Let us go forward determined to serve selflessly a vision of man with God, government for people and humanity at peace. For it is now our task to tend and preserve, through the darkest and, coldest nights, that sacred fire of liberty that President Washington spoke of two centuries ago; fire that tonight remains a beacon to all oppressed of the world, springing forth from this kindly, pleasant land we call America." (President Ronald Reagan)

"There is no institution more vital to our nation's survival than the American family. Here the seeds of personal character are planted, the roots of public virtue first nourished. Through love and instruction, discipline, guidance and example, we learn from our mothers and fathers the values that will shape our private lives and public citizenship."
(President Ronald Reagan)

"Our national motto, "In God we trust", was not chosen lightly. It reflects a basic recognition that there is a divine authority in the universe to which this nation owes homage." (President Ronald Reagan)

"I've always believed that we were, each of us, put here for a reason; that there is a plan; somehow, a divine plan for all of us. I know now that whatever days are left to me, belong to him."
(President Ronald Reagan)

Thanksgiving Proclamation

Issued by President George Washington, at the request of Congress on October 3, 1789

Whereas it is the duty of all nations to acknowledge the providence of Almighty God, to obey His will, to be grateful for His benefits, and humbly to implore His protection and favor; and—Whereas both Houses of Congress have, by their joint committee, requested me "to recommend to the people of the United States a day of public thanksgiving and prayer to be observed by acknowledging with grateful hearts the many and signal favors of Almighty God, especially by affording them an opportunity peaceably to establish a form of government for their safety and happiness.." ,Now, therefore, I do recommend and assign Thursday, the 26th day of November next, to be devoted by the people of these States to the service of that great and glorious Being who is the beneficent author of all the good that was, that is, or that will be; that we may unite in rendering unto Him our sincere and humble thanks for His kind care and protection of the people of this country previous to their becoming a nation; for the signal and manifold mercies and the favorable interpositions of His providence in the course and conclusion of the late war; for the great degree of tranquility, union, and plenty which we have since enjoyed; for the peaceable and rational manner in which we have been enabled to establish constitutions of government for our safety and happiness, and particularly the national one now lately instituted; for the civil and religious liberty with which we are blessed, and the means we have of acquiring and diffusing useful knowledge; and, in general, for all the great and various favors which

He has been pleased to confer upon us. And also that we may then unite in most humbly offering our prayers and supplications to the great Lord and Ruler of Nations, and beseech Him to pardon our national and other transgressions; to enable us all, whether in public or private stations, to perform our several and relative duties properly and punctually; to render our National Government a blessing to all the people by constantly being a Government of wise, just, and constitutional laws, discreetly and faithfully executed and obeyed; to protect and guide all sovereigns and nations (especially such as have shown kindness to us), and to bless them with good government, peace and concord; to promote the knowledge and practice of true religion and virtue, and the increase of science among them and us; and generally, to grant unto all mankind such a degree of temporal prosperity as He alone knows to be best.

Given under my hand at the City of New York the third day of October in the year of our Lord 1789.
(George Washington)

President George Washington

"I believe the Bible is the best gift God has ever given to man. All the good of the Savior of the world is communicated to us through the Book"
(President Abraham Lincoln)

President Abraham Lincoln

Following are several quotes from President Ronald Reagan:

"It was the hard work of our people, the freedom they enjoyed and their faith in God that built this country and made it the envy of the world. In all our great cities and towns, evidence of the faith of our people is found. Houses of worship are among the oldest structures. While never willing to bow to a tyrant, our forefathers were always willing to get on their knees before God. When catastrophe threatened, they turned to God for deliverance. When the harvest was bountiful, the first thought was thanksgiving to God."

Photograph in the Carol M. Highsmith Archive, Library of Congress Prints and Photographs Division

President Ronald Reagan

"Throughout our history, Americans have put their faith in God and no one can doubt that we have been blessed for it. The earliest settlers of this land came in search of religious freedom. Landing on a desolate shoreline, they established a spiritual foundation that has served us ever since."

"Only our deep moral values and our strong social institutions can hold back that jungle and restrain the darker impulses of human nature."

"I also believe this blessed land was set apart in a very special way, a country created by men and women who came here, not in search of gold, but in search of God. They would be free people, living under the law with faith in their maker and their future. Sometimes, it seems we've strayed from that noble beginning, from our conviction that standards of right and wrong do exist and must be lived up to."

"God, the source of our knowledge, has been expelled from the classroom. He gives us His greatest blessing, life, and yet many would condone the taking of innocent life. We expect Him to protect us in a crisis, but turn away from Him too often in our day to day living. I wonder if He isn't waiting for us to wake up."

"It has been written, that the most sublime figure in American history was George Washington on his knees in the snow at Valley Forge. He personified a people who knew that it was not enough to depend on their own courage and goodness, that they must also seek help from God, their Father and Preserver. Where did we begin to lose sight of that noble beginning, of our conviction that standards of right and wrong do exist and must be lived up to? Do we really think we can have it both ways; that God will protect us in a time of crises even as we turn away from Him in our day to day life?"

President George Washington

"The book of St. John tells us that, 'For God so loved the world that he gave his only begotten son that whosoever believes in him should not perish but have everlasting life.' We have God's promise that what we give will be given back many times over. And we also have His promise that we should take regard to our country, 'That if my people who are called by my name humble themselves and pray and seek my face and turn from their wicked ways, then will I hear from heaven and will forgive their sins and heal their land" (II Chronicles 7:14)

"Maybe it's later than we think. Let us go forth from here and rekindle the fire of our faith. Let our wisdom be vindicated by our deeds, and when our work is done, we can say that we have fought the good fight; we have finished the race; we have kept the faith. And we can say someday to our children's children, 'We did all that could be done in the moment that was given us here on earth.'"

"When Americans reach out for values of faith, family and caring for the needy, they're saying, 'We want the word of God. We want to face the future with the Bible." (President Ronald Reagan)

"We're blessed to have its words of strength, comfort and truth. I'm accused of being simplistic at times with some of the problems that confront us, but I've often wondered: within the covers of that single book are all the answers to all the problems that face us today; if we'd only look there. 'The grass withereth, the flowers fadeth, but the word of God shall stand forever.'" (President Ronald Reagan)

"Let us resolve tonight that young Americans will always find there a city of hope in a country that is free. And let us resolve they will say of our day and our generation, that we did keep the faith with our God. That we did act worthy of ourselves. That we did protect and pass on lovingly that shining city on a hill."
(President Ronald Reagan)

As history is recorded in the Bible, Solomon, son of David, King of Israel, became king in his youth and God, in a dream, spoke to him saying, *"Ask for whatever you want me to give you."*

Solomon replied, "But I am only a little child and do not know how to carry out my duties. Your servant is here among the people you have chosen, a great people, too numerous to count or number. Give your servant a discerning heart to govern your people and to distinguish between right and wrong, for who is able to govern this great people of yours?"

The Lord was pleased that Solomon had asked for this and God said, "I will give you a wise and discerning heart, so that there will never have been anyone like you, nor will there ever be." Solomon authored the Proverbs, Ecclesiastics and many other scripts. He was known to be the wisest man ever to live. In his final words, he states, "Now all has been heard; here is the conclusion of the matter; fear God and keep his commandments, for this is the whole duty of man. For God will bring every deed into judgment, including every hidden thing, whether it is good or evil." (Ecc 12:13-14)

Jesus said to John, "Strengthen the things that remain." (Book of Revelations 3:2)

I hope you will be inspired and encouraged as the pages of history continue to unfold. We tell the story of America with our lives and actions, in the future content of that book, because it will be recorded for all time in eternity. Together, and by the grace of God, let's make America right again.

History is being written as each hour passes. What part will we have in its making? We as Americans can participate in shaping the future, not just for ourselves, but for our children too. None of us are insignificant in this role. What will be our legacy in life when we go on to rest with our fathers? I hope and pray that my father in heaven is pleased, and welcomes me into the gates of the city of God. If he says, "Well done my good and faithful servant, enter in" then I will know if I have done well.

Every Child in this nation has the inalienable right to know the truth about American history. We as their peers have an inherent obligation to impart this truth of our founding to our children.

"Righteousness exalts a nation, but sin condemns any people." (Proverbs 11:9)

"The Lord loves righteousness and justice; the earth is full of his unfailing love." (Psalms 33:5)

"Now I, Nebuchadnezzar, praise and exalt and glorify the King of Heaven, because everything he does is right and all his ways are just. And those who walk in pride he is able to humble." (Daniel 4:37)

Make America Right Again!

Janet R. Chipps

Janet R. Chipps

Janet R. Chipps

Janet R. Chipps

Children are a heritage from the Lord,
offspring a reward from him.

Like arrows in the hands of a warrior
are children born in one's youth.

Blessed is the man whose quiver is
full of them.

(Psalm 127:3-5)

Janet R. Chipps

Tim Chipps

Tim Chipps has made his profession in the construction industry for the past 40 years. The father of 19 children, he now resides in Alaska with his wife and family.

APPENDIX

Declaration of Independence

IN CONGRESS, July 4, 1776.

The unanimous Declaration of the thirteen united States of America,

When in the Course of human events, it becomes necessary for one people to dissolve the political bands which have connected them with another, and to assume among the powers of the earth, the separate and equal station to which the Laws of Nature and of Nature's God entitle them, a decent respect to the opinions of mankind requires that they should declare the causes which impel them to the separation.

We hold these truths to be self-evident, that all men are created equal, that they are endowed by their Creator with certain unalienable Rights, that among these are Life, Liberty and the pursuit f Happiness.— That to secure these rights, Governments are instituted among Men, deriving their just powers from the consent of the governed,—That whenever any Form of Government becomes destructive of these ends, it is the Right of the People to alter or to abolish it, and to institute new Government, laying its foundation on such principles and organizing its powers in such form, as to them shall seem most likely to effect their Safety and Happiness. Prudence, indeed, will dictate that Governments long established should not be changed for light and transient causes; and accordingly all experience hath shewn, that mankind are more disposed to suffer, while evils are sufferable, than to right themselves by abolishing the forms to which they are accustomed. But when a long train of abuses and usurpations, pursuing invariably the same Object evinces a design to reduce them under absolute

Despotism, it is their right, it is their duty, to throw off such Government, and to provide new Guards for their future security.— Such has been the patient sufferance of these Colonies; and such is now the necessity which constrains them to alter their former Systems of Government. The history of the present King of Great Britain is a history of repeated injuries and usurpations, all having in direct object the establishment of an absolute Tyranny over these States. To prove this, let Facts be submitted to a candid world.

He has refused his Assent to Laws, the most wholesome and necessary for the public good.

He has forbidden his Governors to pass Laws of immediate and pressing importance, unless suspended in their operation till his Assent should be obtained; and when so suspended, he has utterly neglected to attend to them.

He has refused to pass other Laws for the accommodation of large districts of people, unless those people would relinquish the right of Representation in the Legislature, a right inestimable to them and formidable to tyrants only.

He has called together legislative bodies at places unusual, uncomfortable, and distant from the depository of their public Records, for the sole purpose of fatiguing them into compliance with his measures.

He has dissolved Representative Houses repeatedly, for opposing with manly firmness his invasions on the rights of the people.

He has refused for a long time, after such dissolutions, to cause others to be elected; whereby the Legislative powers, incapable of Annihilation, have returned to the People at large for their exercise; the State remaining in the mean time exposed to all the dangers of invasion from without, and convulsions within.

He has endeavoured to prevent the population of these States; for that purpose obstructing the Laws for Naturalization of Foreigners; refusing to pass others to encourage their migrations hither, and raising the conditions of new Appropriations of Lands.

He has obstructed the Administration of Justice, by refusing his Assent to Laws for establishing Judiciary powers.

He has made Judges dependent on his Will alone, for the tenure of their offices, and the amount and payment of their salaries.

He has erected a multitude of New Offices, and sent hither swarms of Officers to harass our people, and eat out their substance.

He has kept among us, in times of peace, Standing Armies without the Consent of our legislatures.

He has affected to render the Military independent of and superior to the Civil power.

He has combined with others to subject us to a jurisdiction foreign to our constitution, and unacknowledged by our laws; giving his Assent to their Acts of pretended Legislation:

For Quartering large bodies of armed troops among us:

For protecting them, by a mock Trial, from punishment for

any Murders which they should commit on the Inhabitants of these States:

For cutting off our Trade with all parts of the world:

For imposing Taxes on us without our Consent:

For depriving us in many cases, of the benefits of Trial by Jury:

For transporting us beyond Seas to be tried for pretended offences

For abolishing the free System of English Laws in a neighbouring Province, establishing therein an Arbitrary government, and enlarging its Boundaries so as to render it at once an example and fit instrument for introducing the same absolute rule into these Colonies:

For taking away our Charters, abolishing our most valuable Laws, and altering fundamentally the Forms of our Governments:

For suspending our own Legislatures, and declaring themselves invested with power to legislate for us in all cases whatsoever.

He has abdicated Government here, by declaring us out of his Protection and waging War against us.

He has plundered our seas, ravaged our Coasts, burnt our towns, and destroyed the lives of our people.

He is at this time transporting large Armies of foreign Mercenaries to compleat the works of death, desolation and tyranny, already begun with circumstances of Cruelty & perfidy scarcely paralleled in the most barbarous ages, and totally unworthy of the Head of a civilized nation.

He has constrained our fellow Citizens taken Captive on the high Seas to bear arms against their Country, to become the executioners of their friends and Brethren, or to fall themselves by their Hands.

He has excited domestic insurrections amongst us, and has endeavoured to bring on the inhabitants of our frontiers, the merciless Indian Savages, whose known rule of warfare, is an undistinguished destruction of all ages, sexes and conditions.

In every stage of these Oppressions We have Petitioned for Redress in the most humble terms: Our repeated Petitions have been answered only by repeated injury. A Prince whose character is thus marked by every act which may define a Tyrant, is unfit to be the ruler of a free people.

Nor have We been wanting in attentions to our Brittish brethren. We have warned them from time to time of attempts by their legislature to extend an unwarrantable jurisdiction over us. We have reminded them of the circumstances of our emigration and settlement here. We have appealed to their native justice and magnanimity, and we have conjured them by the ties of our common kindred to disavow these usurpations, which, would inevitably interrupt our connections and correspondence. They too have been deaf to the voice of justice and of consanguinity. We must, therefore, acquiesce in the necessity, which denounces our Separation, and hold them, as we hold the rest of mankind, Enemies in War, in Peace Friends.

We, therefore, the Representatives of the united States of America, in General Congress, Assembled, appealing to the Supreme Judge of the world for the rectitude of our intentions, do, in the Name, and by Authority of the good People of these Colonies, solemnly publish and declare, That these United Colonies are, and of Right ought to be Free and Independent States; that they are Absolved from all Allegiance to the British Crown, and that all political connection between them and the State of Great Britain, is and ought to be totally dissolved; and that as Free and Independent States, they have full Power to levy War, conclude Peace, contract Alliances, establish Commerce, and to do all other Acts and Things which Independent States may of right do. And for the support of this Declaration, with a firm reliance on the protection of divine Providence, we mutually pledge to each other our Lives, our Fortunes and our sacred Honor.

Georgia:
Button Gwinnett
Lyman Hall
George Walton
North Carolina:
William Hooper
Joseph Hewes
John Penn
South Carolina:
Edward Rutledge
Thomas Heyward, Jr.
Thomas Lynch, Jr.
Arthur Middleton
Massachusetts:
John Hancock
Maryland:
Samuel Chase
William Paca
Thomas Stone
Charles Carroll of
Carrollton
Virginia:
George Wythe
Richard Henry Lee

Thomas Jefferson
Benjamin Harrison
Thomas Nelson, Jr.
Francis Lightfoot Lee
Carter Braxton
Pennsylvania:
Robert Morris
Benjamin Rush
Benjamin Franklin
John Morton
George Clymer
James Smith
George Taylor
James Wilson
George Ross
Delaware:
Caesar Rodney
George Read
Thomas McKean
New York:
William Floyd
Philip Livingston
Francis Lewis
Lewis Morris

New Jersey:
Richard Stockton
John Witherspoon
Francis Hopkinson
John Hart
Abraham Clark
New Hampshire:
Josiah Bartlett
William Whipple
Massachusetts:
Samuel Adams
John Adams
Robert Treat Paine
Elbridge Gerry
Rhode Island:
Stephen Hopkins
William Ellery
Connecticut:
Roger Sherman
Samuel Huntington
William Williams
Oliver Wolcott
New Hampshire:
Matthew Thornton

CONSTITUTION OF THE UNITED STATES

We the People of the United States, in Order to form a more perfect Union, establish Justice, insure domestic Tranquility, provide for the common defence, promote the general Welfare, and secure the Blessings of Liberty to ourselves and our Posterity, do ordain and establish this Constitution for the United States of America.

Article I.

Section 1. All legislative Powers herein granted shall be vested in a Congress of the United States, which shall consist of a Senate and House of Representatives.

Section 2. The House of Representatives shall be composed of Members chosen every second Year by the People of the several States, and the Electors in each State shall have the Qualifications requisite for Electors of the most numerous Branch of the State Legislature.

No Person shall be a Representative who shall not have attained to the age of twenty five Years, and been seven Years a Citizen of the United States, and who shall not, when elected, be an Inhabitant of that State in which he shall be chosen.

Representatives and direct Taxes shall be apportioned among the several States which may be included within this Union, according to their respective Numbers, which shall be determined by adding to the whole Number of free Persons, including those bound to Service for a Term of Years, and excluding Indians not taxed, three fifths of all other Persons. The actual Enumeration shall be made within three Years after the first Meeting of the Congress of the United States, and within every subsequent Term of ten Years, in such Manner as they shall by Law direct. The Number of Representatives shall not exceed one for every thirty Thousand, but each State shall have at Least one Representative; and until such enumeration shall be made, the State of New Hampshire shall be entitled to chuse three, Massachusetts eight, Rhode Island and Providence Plantations one, Connecticut five, New York six, New Jersey four, Pennsylvania eight, Delaware one, Maryland six, Virginia ten, North Carolina five, South Carolina five, and Georgia three.

When vacancies happen in the Representation from any State, the Executive Authority thereof shall issue Writs of Election to fill such Vacancies.

The House of Representatives shall chuse their Speaker and other Officers; and shall have the sole Power of Impeachment.

Section 3. The Senate of the United States shall be composed of two Senators from each State, chosen by the Legislature thereof, for six Years; and each Senator shall have one Vote.

Immediately after they shall be assembled in Consequence of the first Election, they shall be divided as equally as may be into three Classes. The Seats of the Senators of the first Class shall be vacated at the Expiration of the second Year, of the second Class at the Expiration of the fourth Year, and the third Class at the Expiration of the sixth Year, so that one third may be chosen every second Year; and if Vacancies happen by Resignation, or otherwise, during the Recess of the Legislature of any State, the Executive thereof may make temporary Appointments until the next Meeting of the Legislature, which shall then fill such Vacancies.

No Person shall be a Senator who shall not have attained to the Age of thirty Years, and been nine Years a Citizen of the

United States and who shall not, when elected, be an Inhabitant of that State for which he shall be chosen.

The Vice President of the United States shall be President of the Senate but shall have no Vote, unless they be equally divided.

The Senate shall chuse their other Officers, and also a President *pro tempore*, in the Absence of the Vice President, or when he shall exercise the Office of President of the United States.

The Senate shall have the sole Power to try all Impeachments. When sitting for that Purpose, they shall be on Oath or Affirmation. When the President of the United States is tried the Chief Justice shall preside: And no Person shall be convicted without the Concurrence of two thirds of the Members present.

Judgment in Cases of Impeachment shall not extend further than to removal from Office, and disqualification to hold and enjoy any Office of honor, Trust or Profit under the United States: but the Party convicted shall nevertheless be liable and subject to Indictment, Trial, Judgment and Punishment, according to Law.

Section 4. The Times, Places and Manner of holding Elections for Senators and Representatives, shall be prescribed in each State by the Legislature thereof; but the Congress may at any time by Law make or alter such Regulations, except as to the Places of chusing Senators.

The Congress shall assemble at least once in every Year, and such Meeting shall be on the first Monday in December, unless they shall by Law appoint a different Day.

Section 5. Each House shall be the Judge of the Elections, Returns and Qualifications of its own Members, and a Majority of each shall constitute a Quorum to do Business; but a smaller Number may adjourn from day to day, and may be authorized to compel the Attendance of absent Members, in such Manner, and under such Penalties as each House may provide.

Each House may determine the Rules of its Proceedings, punish its Members for disorderly Behaviour, and, with the Concurrence of two thirds, expel a Member.

Each House shall keep a Journal of its Proceedings, and from time to time publish the same, excepting such Parts as may in their Judgment require Secrecy; and the Yeas and Nays of the Members of either House on any question shall, at the Desire of one fifth of those Present, be entered on the Journal.

Neither House, during the Session of Congress, shall, without the Consent of the other, adjourn for more than three days, nor to any other Place than that in which the two Houses shall be sitting.

Section 6. The Senators and Representatives shall receive a Compensation for their Services, to be ascertained by Law, and paid out of the Treasury of the United States. They shall in all Cases, except Treason, Felony and Breach of the Peace, be privileged from Arrest during their Attendance at the Session of their respective Houses, and in going to and returning from the same; and for any Speech or Debate in either House, they shall not be questioned in any other Place.

No Senator or Representative shall, during the Time for which he was elected, be appointed to any civil Office under the Authority of the United States, which shall have been created, or the

Emoluments whereof shall have been encreased during such time; and no Person holding any Office under the United States, shall be a Member of either House during his Continuance in Office.

Section 7. All Bills for raising Revenue shall originate in the House of Representatives; but the Senate may propose or concur with amendments as on other Bills.

Every Bill which shall have passed the House of Representatives and the Senate, shall, before it become a law, be presented to the President of the United States: If he approve he shall sign it, but if not he shall return it, with his Objections to that House in which it shall have originated, who shall enter the Objections at large on their Journal, and proceed to reconsider it. If after such Reconsideration two thirds of that House shall agree to pass the Bill, it shall be sent, together with the Objections, to the other House, by which it shall likewise be reconsidered, and if approved by two thirds of that House, it shall become a Law. But in all such Cases the Votes of both Houses shall be determined by Yeas and Nays, and the Names of the Persons voting for and against the Bill shall be entered on the Journal of each House respectively. If any Bill shall not be returned by the President within ten Days (Sundays excepted) after it shall have been presented to him, the Same shall be a Law, in like Manner as if he had signed it, unless the Congress by their Adjournment prevent its Return, in which Case it shall not be a Law

Every Order, Resolution, or Vote to which the Concurrence of the Senate and House of Representatives may be necessary (except on a question of Adjournment) shall be presented to the President of the United States; and before the Same shall take

Effect, shall be approved by him, or being disapproved by him, shall be repassed by two thirds of the Senate and House of Representatives, according to the Rules and Limitations prescribed in the Case of a Bill.

Section 8. The Congress shall have Power To lay and collect Taxes, Duties, Imposts and Excises, to pay the Debts and provide for the common Defence and general Welfare of the United States; but all Duties, Imposts and Excises shall be uniform throughout the United States;

To borrow Money on the credit of the United States;

To regulate Commerce with foreign Nations, and among the several States, and with the Indian Tribes;

To establish an uniform Rule of Naturalization, and uniform Laws on the subject of Bankruptcies throughout the United States;

To coin Money, regulate the Value thereof, and of foreign Coin, and fix the Standard of Weights and Measures;

To provide for the Punishment of counterfeiting the Securities and current Coin of the United States;

To establish Post Offices and post Roads;

To promote the Progress of Science and useful Arts, by securing for limited Times to Authors and Inventors the exclusive Right to their respective Writings and Discoveries;

To constitute Tribunals inferior to the supreme Court;

To define and punish Piracies and Felonies committed on the high Seas, and Offences against the Law of Nations;

To declare War, grant Letters of Marque and Reprisal, and make Rules concerning Captures on Land and Water;

To raise and support Armies, but no Appropriation of Money to that Use shall be for a longer Term than two Years;

To provide and maintain a Navy;

To make Rules for the Government and Regulation of the land and naval Forces;

To provide for calling forth the Militia to execute the Laws of the Union, suppress Insurrections and repel Invasions;

To provide for organizing, arming, and disciplining, the Militia, and for governing such Part of them as may be employed in the Service of the United States, reserving to the States respectively, the Appointment of the Officers, and the Authority of training the Militia according to the discipline prescribed by Congress;

To exercise exclusive Legislation in all Cases whatsoever, over such District (not exceeding ten Miles square) as may, by Cession of Particular States, and the Acceptance of Congress, become the seat of the Government of the United States, and to exercise like Authority over all Places purchased by the Consent of the Legislature of the State in which the Same shall be, for the Erection of Forts, Magazines, Arsenals, dock-Yards, and other needful Buildings;—And

To make all Laws which shall be necessary and proper for carrying into Execution the foregoing Powers, and all other Powers vested by this Constitution in the Government of the United States, or in any Department or Officer thereof.

Section 9. The Migration or Importation of such Persons as any of the States now existing shall think proper to admit, shall not be prohibited by the Congress prior to the Year one thousand eight hundred and eight, but a Tax or duty may be imposed on such Importation, not exceeding ten dollars for each Person.

The Privilege of the Writ of *Habeas Corpus* shall not be suspended, unless when in Cases or Rebellion or Invasion the public Safety may require it.

No Bill of Attainder or *ex post facto* Law shall be passed.

No Capitation, or other direct, Tax shall be laid, unless in the Proportion to the Census of Enumeration herein before directed to be taken.

No Tax or Duty shall be laid on Articles exported from any State.

No Preference shall be given by any Regulation of Commerce or Revenue to the Ports of one State over those of another: nor shall Vessels bound to, or from, one State, be obliged to enter, clear or pay Duties in another.

No Money shall be drawn from the Treasury, but in Consequence of Appropriations made by Law; and a regular Statement and Account of the Receipts and Expenditures of all public Money shall be published from time to time.

No Title of Nobility shall be granted by the United States: and no Person holding any Office of Profit or Trust under them, shall, without the Consent of the Congress, accept of any present, Emolument, Office, or Title, of any kind whatever, from any King, Prince, or foreign State.

Section 10. No State shall enter into any Treaty, Alliance, or Confederation; grant Letters of Marque and Reprisal; coin Money; emit Bills of Credit; make any Thing but gold and silver Coin a Tender in Payment of Debts; pass any Bill of Attainder, *ex post facto* Law, or Law impairing the Obligation of Contracts, or grant any Title of Nobility.

No State shall, without the Consent of the Congress, lay any Imposts or Duties on Imports or Exports, except what may be absolutely necessary for executing it's inspection Laws: and the net Produce of all Duties and Imposts, laid by any State on Imports or Exports, shall be for the Use of the Treasury of the United States; and all such Laws shall be subject to the Revision and Controul of the Congress.

No State shall, without the Consent of Congress, lay any Duty of Tonnage, keep Troops, or Ships of War in time of Peace, enter into any Agreement or Compact with another State, or with a foreign Power, or engage in War, unless actually invaded, or in such imminent Danger as will not admit of delay.

Article II.

Section 1. The executive Power shall be vested in a President of the United States of America. He shall hold his Office during the Term of four Years, and, together with the Vice President, chosen for the same Term, be elected, as follows:

Each State shall appoint, in such Manner as the Legislature thereof may direct, a Number of Electors, equal to the whole Number of Senators and Representatives to which the State may be entitled in the Congress: but no Senator or Representative, or Person holding an Office of Trust or Profit under the United States, shall be appointed an Elector.

The Electors shall meet in their respective States, and vote by Ballot for two Persons, of whom one at least shall not be an Inhabitant of the same State with themselves. And they shall make a List of all the Persons voted for, and of the Number of Votes for each; which List they shall sign and certify, and transmit sealed to the Seat of the Government of the United States, directed to the President of the Senate. The President of the Senate shall, in the Presence of the Senate and House of Representatives, open all the Certificates, and the Votes shall then be counted. The Person having the greatest Number of Votes shall be the President, if such Number be a Majority of the whole Number of Electors appointed; and if there be more than one who have such Majority, and have an equal Number of Votes, then the House of Representatives shall immediately chuse by Ballot one of them for President; and if no Person have a Majority, then from the five highest on the List the said House shall in like Manner chuse the President. But in chusing the President, the Votes shall be taken by States, the Representatives from each State having one Vote; a quorum for this Purpose shall consist of a Member or Members from two thirds of the States, and a Majority of all the States shall be necessary to a Choice. In every Case, after the Choice of the President, the Person having the greatest Number of Votes of the Electors shall be the Vice President. But if there should remain two or more who have equal Votes, the Senate shall chuse from them by Ballot the Vice President.

The Congress may determine the Time of chusing the Electors, and the Day on which they shall give their Votes; which Day shall be the same throughout the United States.

No Person except a natural born Citizen, or a Citizen of the United States, at the time of the Adoption of this Constitution, shall be eligible to the Office of President; neither shall any person be eligible to that Office who shall not have attained to the Age of thirty five Years, and been fourteen Years a Resident within the United States.

In Case of the Removal of the President from Office, or of his Death, Resignation, or Inability to discharge the Powers and

Duties of the said Office, the Same shall devolve on the Vice President, and the Congress may by Law provide for the Case of Removal, Death, Resignation or Inability, both of the President and Vice President, declaring what Officer shall then act as President, and such Officer shall act accordingly, until the Disability be removed, or a President shall be elected.

The President shall, at stated Times, receive for his Services, a Compensation, which shall neither be encreased nor diminished during the Period for which he shall have been elected, and he shall not receive within that Period any other Emolument from the United States, or any of them.

Before he enter on the Execution of his Office, he shall take the following Oath or Affirmation:—"I do solemnly swear (or affirm) that I will faithfully execute the Office of President of the United States, and will to the best of my Ability, preserve, protect and defend the Constitution of the United States."

Section 2. The President shall be Commander in Chief of the Army and Navy of the United States, and of the Militia of the several States, when called into the actual Service of the United States; he may require the Opinion, in writing, of the principal Officer in each of the executive Departments, upon any Subject relating to the Duties of their respective Offices, and he shall have Power to Grant Reprieves and Pardons for Offences against the United States, except in Cases of Impeachment.

He shall have Power, by and with the Advice and Consent of the Senate, to make Treaties, provided two thirds of the Senators present concur; and he shall nominate, and by and with the Advice and Consent of the Senate, shall appoint Ambassadors, other public Ministers and Consuls, Judges of the supreme Court, and all other Officers of the United States, whose Appointments are not herein otherwise provided for, and which shall be established by Law: but the Congress may by Law vest the Appointment of such inferior Officers, as they think proper, in the President alone, in the Courts of Law, or in the Heads of Departments.

The President shall have Power to fill up all Vacancies that may happen during the Recess of the Senate, by granting Commissions which shall expire at the End of their next Session.

Section 3. He shall from time to time give to the Congress Information on the State of the Union, and recommend to their Consideration such Measures as he shall judge necessary and expedient; he may, on extraordinary Occasions, convene both Houses, or either of them, and in Case of Disagreement between them, with Respect to the Time of Adjournment, he may adjourn them to such Time as he shall think proper; he shall receive Ambassadors and other public Ministers; he shall take Care that the Laws be faithfully executed, and shall Commission all the Officers of the United States.

Section 4. The President, Vice President and all Civil Officers of the United States, shall be removed from Office on Impeachment for and Conviction of, Treason, Bribery, or other high Crimes and Misdemeanors.

Article III.

Section 1. The judicial Power of the United States, shall be vested in one supreme Court, and in such inferior Courts as the Congress may from time to time ordain and establish. The Judges, both of the supreme and inferior Courts, shall hold their Offices during good Behaviour, and shall, at stated Times, receive for their Services, a Compensation, which shall not be diminished during their Continuance in Office.

Section 2. The judicial Power shall extend to all Cases, in Law and Equity, arising under this Constitution, the Laws of the United States, and Treaties made, or which shall be made, under their Authority;—to all Cases affecting Ambassadors, other public ministers and Consuls;—to all Cases of admiralty and maritime Jurisdiction;—to Controversies to which the United States shall be a Party;—to Controversies between two or more States;— between a State and Citizens of another State;— between Citizens of different States;—between Citizens of the same State claiming Lands under Grants of different States, and between a State, or the Citizens thereof, and foreign States, Citizens or Subjects.

In all Cases affecting Ambassadors, other public Ministers and Consuls, and those in which a State shall be Party, the supreme Court shall have original Jurisdiction. In all the other Cases before mentioned, the supreme Court shall have appellate Jurisdiction, both as to Law and Fact, with such Exceptions, and under such Regulations as the Congress shall make.

The Trial of all Crimes, except in Cases of Impeachment, shall be by Jury; and such Trial shall be held in the State where the said Crimes shall have been committed; but when not committed within any State, the Trial shall be at such Place or Places as the Congress may by Law have directed.

Section 3. Treason against the United States, shall consist only in levying War against them, or in adhering to their Enemies, giving them Aid and Comfort. No Person shall be convicted of Treason unless on the Testimony of two Witnesses to the same overt Act, or on Confession in open Court.

The Congress shall have Power to declare the Punishment of Treason, but no Attainder of Treason shall work Corruption of Blood, or Forfeiture except during the Life of the Person attainted.

Article IV.

Section 1. Full Faith and Credit shall be given in each State to the public Acts, Records, and judicial Proceedings of every other State. And the Congress may by general Laws prescribe the Manner in which such Acts, Records, and Proceedings shall be proved, and the Effect thereof.

Section 2. The Citizens of each State shall be entitled to all Privileges and Immunities of Citizens in the several States.

A Person charged in any State with Treason, Felony, or other Crime, who shall flee from Justice, and be found in another State, shall on Demand of the executive Authority of the State from which he fled, be delivered up, to be removed to the State having Jurisdiction of the Crime.

No Person held to Service or Labour in one State, under the Laws thereof, escaping into another, shall, in Consequence of any Law or Regulation therein, be discharged from such Service or Labour, but shall be delivered up on Claim of the Party to whom such Service or Labour may be due.

Section 3. New States may be admitted by the Congress into this Union; but no new State shall be formed or erected within the Jurisdiction of any other State; nor any State be formed by the Junction of two or more States, or Parts of States, without the Consent of the Legislatures of the States concerned as well as of the Congress.

The Congress shall have Power to dispose of and make all needful Rules and Regulations respecting the Territory or other Property belonging to the United States; and nothing in this Constitution shall be so construed as to Prejudice any Claims of the United States, or of any particular State.

Section 4. The United States shall guarantee to every State in this Union a Republican Form of Government, and shall protect each of them against Invasion; and on Application of the Legislature, or of the Executive (when the Legislature cannot be convened) against domestic Violence.

Article V.

The Congress, whenever two thirds of both Houses shall deem it necessary, shall propose Amendments to this Constitution, or, on the Application of the Legislatures of two thirds of the several States, shall call a Convention for proposing Amendments, which, in either Case, shall be valid to all Intents and Purposes, as Part of this Constitution, when ratified by the Legislatures of three fourths of the several States, or by Conventions in three fourths thereof, as the one or the other Mode of Ratification may be proposed by the Congress; Provided that no Amendment which may be made prior to the Year One thousand eight hundred and eight shall in any Manner affect the first and fourth Clauses in the Ninth Section of the first Article; and that no State, without its Consent, shall be deprived of its equal Suffrage in the Senate.

Article VI.

All Debts contracted and Engagements entered into, before the Adoption of this Constitution, shall be as valid against the United States under this Constitution, as under the Confederation.

This Constitution, and the Laws of the United States which shall be made in Pursuance thereof; and all Treaties made, or which shall be made, under the Authority of the United States, shall be the supreme Law of the Land; and the Judges in every State shall be bound thereby, any Thing in the Constitution or Laws of any state to the Contrary notwithstanding.

The Senators and Representatives before mentioned, and the Members of the several State Legislatures, and all executive and judicial Officers, both of the United States and of the several States, shall be bound by Oath or Affirmation, to support this Constitution; but no religious Test shall ever be required as a Qualification to any Office or public Trust under the United States.

Article VII.

The Ratification of the Conventions of nine States, shall be sufficient for the Establishment of this Constitution between the States so ratifying the same.

The Word, "the," being inter-lined between the seventh and eighth Lines of the first Page, The Word "Thirty" being partly written on an Erazure in the fifteenth Line of the first Page, The Words "is tried" being inter-lined between the thirty second and thirty third Lines of the first Page and the Word "the" being interlined between the forty third and forty fourth Lines of the second Page.

Attest WILLIAM JACKSON
Secretary

done in Convention by the Unanimous Consent of the States present the Seventeenth Day of September in the Year of our Lord one thousand seven hundred and Eighty seven and of the Independance of the United States of America the Twelfth. In witness whereof We have hereunto subscribed our Names,

G⁰. WASHINGTON—Presidᵗ.
and deputy from Virginia

New Hampshire   JOHN LANGDON
                  NICHOLAS GILMAN

Massachusetts   NATHANIEL GORHAM
                  RUFUS KING

Connecticut	Wm Saml Johnson Roger Sherman
New York	Alexander Hamilton
New Jersey	Wil: Livingston David Brearley. Wm Patterson. Jona: Dayton
Pennsylvania	B Franklin Thomas Mifflin Robt Morris Geo. Clymer Thos FitzSimons Jared Ingersol James Wilson Gouv Morris
Delaware	Geo: Read Gunning Bedford Jun John Dickinson Richard Bassett Jaco: Broom
Maryland	James McHenry Dan of St Thos Jenifer Danl Carroll
Virginia	John Blair— James Madison Jr.
North Carolina	Wm Blount Richd Dobbs Spaight Hu Williamson
South Carolina	J. Rutledge Charles Cotesworth Pinckney Charles Pinckney Pierce Butler
Georgia	William Few Abr Baldwin

In Convention Monday, September 17th 1787.

Present

The States of

New Hampshire, Massachusetts, Connecticut, Mr Hamilton from New York, New Jersey, Pennsylvania, Delaware, Maryland, Virginia, North Carolina, South Carolina and Georgia.

Resolved,

That the preceeding Constitution be laid before the United States in Congress assembled, and that it is the Opinion of this Convention, that it should afterwards be submitted to a Convention of Delegates, chosen in each State by the People thereof, under the Recommendation of its Legislature, for their Assent and Ratification; and that each Convention assenting to, and ratifying the Same, should give Notice thereof to the United States in Congress assembled. Resolved, That it is the Opinion of this Convention, that as soon as the Conventions of nine States shall have ratified this Constitution, the United States in Congress assembled should fix a Day on which Electors should be appointed by the States which shall have ratified the same, and a Day on which the Electors should assemble to vote for the President, and the Time and Place for commencing Proceedings under this Constitution. That after such Publication the Electors should be appointed, and the Senators and Representatives elected: That the Electors should meet on the Day fixed for the Election of the President, and should transmit their Votes certified, signed, sealed and directed, as the Constitution requires, to the Secretary of the United States in Congress assembled, that the Senators and Representatives should convene at the Time and Place assigned; that the Senators should appoint a President of the Senate, for the sole Purpose of receiving, opening and counting the Votes for President; and, that after he shall be chosen, the Congress, together with the President, should, without Delay, proceed to execute this Constitution.

By the Unanimous Order of the Convention

G⁰: WASHINGTON—Presidᵗ.

W. JACKSON Secretary.

The Bill of Rights—Simplified

The first ten amendments to the Constitution are commonly known as The Bill of Rights. The following is a simplified version of the Bill of Rights.

First Amendment
Freedom of Religion, Speech, Press, Assembly, Right to Petition

Second Amendment
Right to keep and bear arms

Third Amendment
No quartering of soldiers

Fourth Amendment
Freedom from unreasonable searches and seizures

Fifth Amendment
Right to due process of law, freedom from self-incrimination, double jeopardy

Sixth Amendment
Rights of accused persons, e.g., right to a speedy and public trial

Seventh Amendment
Right of trial by jury in civil cases

Eighth Amendment
Freedom from excessive bail, cruel and unusual punishments

Ninth Amendment
Other rights of the people

Tenth Amendment
Powers reserved to the states

The Amendments

The following are the Amendments to the Constitution. The first ten Amendments collectively are commonly known as the Bill of Rights.

Amendment 1 - Freedom of Religion, Press, Expression. Ratified 12/15/1791.

Congress shall make no law respecting an establishment of religion, or prohibiting the free exercise thereof; or abridging the freedom of speech, or of the press; or the right of the people peaceably to assemble, and to petition the Government for a redress of grievances.

Amendment 2 - Right to Bear Arms. Ratified 12/15/1791.

A well regulated Militia, being necessary to the security of a free State, the right of the people to keep and bear Arms, shall not be infringed.

Amendment 3 - Quartering of Soldiers. Ratified 12/15/1791.

No Soldier shall, in time of peace be quartered in any house, without the consent of the Owner, nor in time of war, but in a manner to be prescribed by law.

Amendment 4 - Search and Seizure. Ratified 12/15/1791.

The right of the people to be secure in their persons, houses, papers, and effects, against unreasonable searches and seizures, shall not be violated, and no Warrants shall issue, but upon probable cause, supported by Oath or affirmation, and particularly describing the place to be searched, and the persons or things to be seized.

Amendment 5 - Trial and Punishment, Compensation for Takings. Ratified 12/15/1791.

No person shall be held to answer for a capital, or otherwise infamous crime, unless on a presentment or indictment of a Grand Jury, except in cases arising in the land or naval forces, or in the Militia, when in actual service in time of War or public danger; nor shall any person be subject for the same offense to be twice put in jeopardy of life or limb; nor shall be compelled in any criminal case to be a witness against himself, nor be deprived of life, liberty, or property, without due process of law; nor shall private property be taken for public use, without just compensation.

Amendment 6 - Right to Speedy Trial, Confrontation of Witnesses. Ratified 12/15/1791.

In all criminal prosecutions, the accused shall enjoy the right to a speedy and public trial, by an impartial jury of the State and district wherein the crime shall have been committed, which district shall have been previously ascertained by law, and to be informed of the nature and cause of the accusation; to be confronted with the witnesses against him; to have compulsory process for obtaining witnesses in his favor, and to have the Assistance of Counsel for his defence.

Amendment 7 - Trial by Jury in Civil Cases. Ratified 12/15/1791.

In Suits at common law, where the value in controversy shall exceed twenty dollars, the right of trial by jury shall be preserved, and no fact tried by a jury, shall be otherwise re-examined in any Court of the United States, than according to the rules of the common law.

Amendment 8 - Cruel and Unusual Punishment. Ratified 12/15/1791.

Excessive bail shall not be required, nor excessive fines imposed, nor cruel and unusual punishments inflicted.

Amendment 9 - Construction of Constitution. Ratified 12/15/1791.

The enumeration in the Constitution, of certain rights, shall not be construed to deny or disparage others retained by the people.

Amendment 10 - Powers of the States and People. Ratified 12/15/1791.

The powers not delegated to the United States by the Constitution, nor prohibited by it to the States, are reserved to the States respectively, or to the people.

Amendment 11 - Judicial Limits. Ratified 2/7/1795.

The Judicial power of the United States shall not be construed to extend to any suit in law or equity, commenced or prosecuted against one of the United States by Citizens of another State, or by Citizens or Subjects of any Foreign State.

Amendment 12 - Choosing the President, Vice-President. Ratified 6/15/1804.

The Electors shall meet in their respective states, and vote by ballot for President and Vice-President, one of whom, at least, shall not be an inhabitant of the same state with themselves; they shall name in their ballots the person voted for as President, and in distinct ballots the person voted for as Vice-President, and they shall make distinct lists of all persons voted for as President, and of all persons voted for as Vice-President and of the number of votes for each, which lists they shall sign and certify, and transmit sealed to the seat of the government of the United States, directed to the President of the Senate;

The President of the Senate shall, in the presence of the Senate and House of Representatives, open all the certificates and the votes shall then be counted;

The person having the greatest Number of votes for President, shall be the President, if such number be a majority of the whole number of Electors appointed; and if no person have such majority, then from the persons having the highest numbers not exceeding three on the list of those voted for as President, the House of Representatives shall choose immediately, by ballot, the President. But in choosing the President, the votes shall be taken by states, the representation from each state having one vote; a quorum for this purpose shall consist of a member or members from two-thirds of the states, and a majority of all the states shall be necessary to a choice. And if the House of Representatives shall not choose a President whenever the right of choice shall devolve upon them, before the fourth day of March next following, then the Vice-President shall act as President, as in the case of the death or other constitutional disability of the President.

The person having the greatest number of votes as Vice-President, shall be the Vice-President, if such number be a majority of the whole number of Electors appointed, and if no person have a majority, then from the two highest numbers on the list, the Senate shall choose the Vice-President; a quorum for the purpose shall consist of two-thirds of the whole number of Senators, and a majority of the whole number shall be necessary to a choice. But no person constitutionally ineligible to the office of President shall be eligible to that of Vice-President of the United States.

Amendment 13 - Slavery Abolished. Ratified 12/6/1865.

1. Neither slavery nor involuntary servitude, except as a punishment for crime whereof the party shall have been duly convicted, shall exist within the United States, or any place subject to their jurisdiction.

2. Congress shall have power to enforce this article by appropriate legislation.

Amendment 14 - Citizenship Rights. Ratified 7/9/1868.

1. All persons born or naturalized in the United States, and subject to the jurisdiction thereof, are citizens of the United States and of the State wherein they reside. No State shall make or enforce any law which shall abridge the privileges or immunities of citizens of the United States; nor shall any State deprive any person of life, liberty, or property, without due process of law; nor deny to any person within its jurisdiction the equal protection of the laws.

2. Representatives shall be apportioned among the several States according to their respective numbers, counting the whole number of persons in each State, excluding Indians not taxed. But when the right to vote at any election for the choice of electors for President and Vice-President of the United States, Representatives in Congress, the Executive and Judicial officers of a State, or the members of the Legislature thereof, is denied to any of the male inhabitants of such State, being twenty-one years of age, and citizens of the United States, or in any way abridged, except for participation in rebellion, or other crime, the basis of representation therein shall be reduced in the proportion which the number of such male citizens shall bear to the whole number of male citizens twenty-one years of age in such State.

3. No person shall be a Senator or Representative in Congress, or elector of President and Vice-President, or hold any office, civil or military, under the United States, or under any State, who, having previously taken an oath, as a member of Congress, or as an officer of the United States, or as a member of any State legislature, or as an executive or judicial officer of any State, to support the Constitution of the United States, shall have engaged in insurrection or rebellion against the same, or given aid or comfort to the enemies thereof. But Congress may by a vote of two-thirds of each House, remove such disability.

4. The validity of the public debt of the United States, authorized by law, including debts incurred for payment of pensions and bounties for services in suppressing insurrection or rebellion, shall not be questioned. But neither the United States nor any State shall assume or pay any debt or obligation incurred in aid of insurrection or rebellion against the United States, or any claim for the loss or emancipation of any slave; but all such debts, obligations and claims shall be held illegal and void.

5. The Congress shall have power to enforce, by appropriate legislation, the provisions of this article.

Amendment 15 - Race No Bar to Vote. Ratified 2/3/1870.

1. The right of citizens of the United States to vote shall not be denied or abridged by the United States or by any State on account of race, color, or previous condition of servitude.

2. The Congress shall have power to enforce this article by appropriate legislation.

Amendment 16 - Status of Income Tax Clarified. Ratified 2/3/1913.

The Congress shall have power to lay and collect taxes on incomes, from whatever source derived, without apportionment among the several States, and without regard to any census or enumeration.

Amendment 17 - Senators Elected by Popular Vote. Ratified 4/8/1913.

The Senate of the United States shall be composed of two Senators from each State, elected by the people thereof, for six years; and each Senator shall have one vote. The electors in each State shall have the qualifications requisite for electors of the most numerous branch of the State legislatures.

When vacancies happen in the representation of any State in the Senate, the executive authority of such State shall issue writs of election to fill such vacancies: Provided, That the legislature of any State may empower the executive thereof to make temporary appointments until the people fill the vacancies by election as the legislature may direct.

This amendment shall not be so construed as to affect the election or term of any Senator chosen before it becomes valid as part of the Constitution.

Amendment 18 - Liquor Abolished. Ratified 1/16/1919. Repealed by Amendment 21, 12/5/1933.

1. After one year from the ratification of this article the manufacture, sale, or transportation of intoxicating liquors within, the importation thereof into, or the exportation thereof from the United States and all territory subject to the jurisdiction thereof for beverage purposes is hereby prohibited.

2. The Congress and the several States shall have concurrent power to enforce this article by appropriate legislation.

3. This article shall be inoperative unless it shall have been ratified as an amendment to the Constitution by the legislatures of the several States, as provided in the Constitution, within seven years from the date of the submission hereof to the States by the Congress.

Amendment 19 - Women's Suffrage. Ratified 8/18/1920.

The right of citizens of the United States to vote shall not be denied or abridged by the United States or by any State on account of sex.

Congress shall have power to enforce this article by appropriate legislation.

Amendment 20 - Presidential, Congressional Terms. Ratified 1/23/1933.

1. The terms of the President and Vice President shall end at noon on the 20th day of January, and the terms of Senators and Representatives at noon on the 3d day of January, of the years in which such terms would have ended if this article had not been ratified; and the terms of their successors shall then begin.

2. The Congress shall assemble at least once in every year, and such meeting shall begin at noon on the 3d day of January, unless they shall by law appoint a different day.

3. If, at the time fixed for the beginning of the term of the President, the President elect shall have died, the Vice President elect shall become President. If a President shall not have been chosen before the time fixed for the beginning of his term, or if the President elect shall have failed to qualify, then the Vice President elect shall act as President until a President shall have qualified; and the Congress may by law provide for the case wherein neither a President elect nor a Vice President elect shall have qualified, declaring who shall then act as President, or the manner in which one who is to act shall be selected, and such person shall act accordingly until a President or Vice President shall have qualified.

4. The Congress may by law provide for the case of the death of any of the persons from whom the House of Representatives may choose a President whenever the right of choice shall have devolved upon them, and for the case of the death of any of the persons from whom the Senate may choose a Vice President whenever the right of choice shall have devolved upon them.

5. Sections 1 and 2 shall take effect on the 15th day of October following the ratification of this article.

6. This article shall be inoperative unless it shall have been ratified as an amendment to the Constitution by the legislatures of three-fourths of the several States within seven years from the date of its submission.

Amendment 21 - Amendment 18 Repealed. Ratified 12/5/1933.

1. The eighteenth article of amendment to the Constitution of the United States is hereby repealed.

2. The transportation or importation into any State, Territory, or possession of the United States for delivery or use therein of intoxicating liquors, in violation of the laws thereof, is hereby prohibited.

3. The article shall be inoperative unless it shall have been ratified as an amendment to the Constitution by conventions in the several States, as provided in the Constitution, within seven years from the date of the submission hereof to the States by the Congress.

Amendment 22 - Presidential Term Limits. Ratified 2/27/1951.

1. No person shall be elected to the office of the President more than twice, and no person who has held the office of President, or acted as President, for more than two years of a term to which some other person was elected President shall be elected to the office of the President more than once. But this Article shall not apply to any person holding the office of President, when this Article was proposed by the Congress, and shall not prevent any person who may be holding the office of President, or acting as President, during the term within which this Article becomes operative from holding the office of President or acting as President during the remainder of such term.

2. This article shall be inoperative unless it shall have been ratified as an amendment to the Constitution by the legislatures of three-fourths of the several States within seven years from the date of its submission to the States by the Congress.

Amendment 23 - Presidential Vote for District of Columbia. Ratified 3/29/1961.

1. The District constituting the seat of Government of the United States shall appoint in such manner as the Congress may direct: A number of electors of President and Vice President equal to the whole number of Senators and Representatives in Congress to which the District would be entitled if it were a State, but in no event more than the least populous State; they shall be in addition to those appointed by the States, but they shall be considered, for the purposes of the election of President and Vice President, to be electors appointed by a State; and they shall meet in the District and perform such duties as provided by the twelfth article of amendment.

2. The Congress shall have power to enforce this article by appropriate legislation.

Amendment 24 - Poll Tax Barred. Ratified 1/23/1964.

1. The right of citizens of the United States to vote in any primary or other election for President or Vice President, for electors for President or Vice President, or for Senator or

Representative in Congress, shall not be denied or abridged by the United States or any State by reason of failure to pay any poll tax or other tax.

2. The Congress shall have power to enforce this article by appropriate legislation.

Amendment 25 - Presidential Disability and Succession. Ratified 2/10/1967.

1. In case of the removal of the President from office or of his death or resignation, the Vice President shall become President.

2. Whenever there is a vacancy in the office of the Vice President, the President shall nominate a Vice President who shall take office upon confirmation by a majority vote of both Houses of Congress.

3. Whenever the President transmits to the President pro tempore of the Senate and the Speaker of the House of Representatives his written declaration that he is unable to discharge the powers and duties of his office, and until he transmits to them a written declaration to the contrary, such powers and duties shall be discharged by the Vice President as Acting President.

4. Whenever the Vice President and a majority of either the principal officers of the executive departments or of such other body as Congress may by law provide, transmit to the President pro tempore of the Senate and the Speaker of the House of Representatives their written declaration that the President is unable to discharge the powers and duties of his office, the Vice President shall immediately assume the powers and duties of the office as Acting President.

Thereafter, when the President transmits to the President pro tempore of the Senate and the Speaker of the House of Representatives his written declaration that no inability exists, he shall resume the powers and duties of his office unless the Vice President and a majority of either the principal officers of the executive department or of such other body as Congress may by law provide, transmit within four days to the President pro tempore of the Senate and the Speaker of the House of Representatives their written declaration that the President is unable to discharge the powers and duties of his office. Thereupon Congress shall decide the issue, assembling within forty eight hours for that purpose if not in session. If the Congress, within twenty one days after receipt of the latter written declaration, or, if Congress is not in session, within twenty one days after Congress is required to assemble, determines by two thirds vote of both Houses that the President is unable to discharge the powers and duties of his office, the Vice President shall continue to discharge the same as Acting President; otherwise, the President shall resume the powers and duties of his office.

Amendment 26 - Voting Age Set to 18 Years. Ratified 7/1/1971.

1. The right of citizens of the United States, who are eighteen years of age or older, to vote shall not be denied or abridged by the United States or by any State on account of age.

2. The Congress shall have power to enforce this article by appropriate legislation.

Amendment 27 - Limiting Congressional Pay Increases. Ratified 5/7/1992.

No law, varying the compensation for the services of the Senators and Representatives, shall take effect, until an election of Representatives shall have intervened.

Senators of the 115th Congress

ALASKA

Murkowski, Lisa - (R - AK)
522 Hart Senate Office Building Washington DC 20510
(202) 224-6665
Contact: www.murkowski.senaate.gov/public/index.cfm/contact

Sullivan, Dan - (R - AK)
702 Hart Senate Office Building Washington DC 20510 (202) 224-3004
Contact: www.sullivan.senate.gov/contact/email

ALABAMA

Shelby, Richard C. - (R - AL)
304 Russell Senate Office Building Washington DC 20510
(202) 224-5744
Contact: www.shelby.senate.gov/public/index.cfm/emailsenatorshelby

Strange, Luther - (R - AL)
326 Russell Senate Office Building Washington DC 20510
(202) 224-4124
Contact: www.strange.senate.gov/content/contact-senator

ARKANSAS

Boozman, John - (R - AR)
141 Hart Senate Office Building Washington DC 20510
(202) 224-4843
Contact: www.boozman.senate.gov/public/index.cfm/contact

Cotton, Tom - (R - AR)
124 Russell Senate Office Building Washington DC 20510
(202) 224-2353
Contact: www.cotton.senate.gov/?p=contact

ARIZONA

Flake, Jeff - (R - AZ)
413 Russell Senate Office Building Washington DC 20510
(202) 224-4521
Contact: www.flake.senate.gov/public/index.cfm/contact-jeff

ARIZONA cont.

McCain, John - (R - AZ)
218 Russell Senate Office Building Washington DC 20510
(202) 224-2235
Contact: www.mccain.senate.gov/public/index.cfm/contact-form

CALIFORNIA

Feinstein, Dianne - (D - CA)
331 Hart Senate Office Building Washington DC 20510
(202) 224-3841
Contact: www.feinstein.senate.gov/public/index.cfm/e-mail-me

Harris, Kamala D. - (D - CA)
112 Hart Senate Office Building Washington DC 20510 (202) 224-3553
Contact: www.harris.senate.gov/content/contact-senator

COLORADO

Bennet, Michael F. - (D - CO)
261 Russell Senate Office Building Washington DC 20510
(202) 224-5852
Contact: www.bennet.senate.gov/?p=contact

Gardner, Cory - (R - CO)
354 Russell Senate Office Building Washington DC 20510
(202) 224-5941
Contact: www.gardner.senate.gov/contact-cory/email-cory

CONNECTICUT

Blumenthal, Richard - (D - CT)
706 Hart Senate Office Building Washington DC 20510
202) 224-2823
Contact: www.blumenthal.senate.gov/contact/

Murphy, Christopher - (D - CT)
136 Hart Senate Office Building Washington DC 20510 (202) 224-4041
Contact: www.murphy.senate.gov/contact

DELAWARE

Carper, Thomas R. - (D - DE)
513 Hart Senate Office Building Washington DC 20510
(202) 224-2441
Contact: www.carper.senate.gov/public/index.cfm/email-senator-carper

Coons, Christopher A. - (D - DE)
127A Russell Senate Office Building Washington DC 20510
(202) 224-5042
Contact: www.coons.senate.gov/contact

FLORIDA

Nelson, Bill - (D - FL)
716 Hart Senate Office Building Washington DC 20510
(202) 224-5274
Contact: www.billnelson.senate.gov/contact-bill

Rubio, Marco - (R - FL)
284 Russell Senate Office Building Washington DC 20510
(202) 224-3041
Contact: www.rubio.senate.gov/public/index.cfm/contact

GEORGIA

Isakson, Johnny - (R - GA)
131 Russell Senate Office Building Washington DC 20510
(202) 224-3643
Contact: www.isakson.senate.gov/public/index.cfm/email-me

Perdue, David - (R - GA)
455 Russell Senate Office Building Washington DC 20510
(202) 224-3521
Contact: www.perdue.senate.gov/connect/email

HAWAII

Hirono, Mazie K. - (D - HI)
730 Hart Senate Office Building Washington DC 20510 (202) 224-6361
Contact: www.hirono.senate.gov/contact

Schatz, Brian - (D - HI)
722 Hart Senate Office Building Washington DC 20510
(202) 224-3934
Contact: www.schatz.senate.gov/contact

IOWA

Ernst, Joni - (R - IA)
111 Russell Senate Office Building Washington DC 20510
(202) 224-3254
Contact: www.ernst.senate.gov/public/index.cfm/contact

IOWA cont.

Grassley, Chuck - (R - IA)
135 Hart Senate Office Building Washington DC 20510
(202) 224-3744
Contact: www.grassley.senate.gov/contact

IDAHO

Crapo, Mike - (R - ID)
239 Dirksen Senate Office Building Washington DC 20510
(202) 224-6142
Contact: www.crapo.senate.gov/contact

Risch, James E. - (R - ID)
483 Russell Senate Office Building Washington DC 20510
(202) 224-2752
Contact: www.risch.senate.gov/public/index.cfm?p=Email

ILLINOIS

Duckworth, Tammy - (D - IL)
524 Hart Senate Office Building Washington DC 20510
(202) 224-2854
Contact: www.duckworth.senate.gov/content/contact-senator

Durbin, Richard J. - (D - IL)
711 Hart Senate Office Building Washington DC 20510 (202) 224-2152
Contact: www.durbin.senate.gov/contact/

INDIANA

Donnelly, Joe - (D - IN)
720 Hart Senate Office Building Washington DC 20510
(202) 224-4814
Contact: www.donnelly.senate.gov/contact/email-joe

Young, Todd - (R - IN)
400 Russell Senate Office Building Washington DC 20510
(202) 224-5623
Contact: www.young.senate.gov/content/contact-senator

KANSAS

Moran, Jerry - (R - KS)
521 Dirksen Senate Office Building Washington DC 20510
(202) 224-6521
Contact: www.moran.senate.gov/public/index.cfm/e-mail-jerry

Roberts, Pat - (R - KS)
109 Hart Senate Office Building Washington DC 20510
(202) 224-4774
Contact: www.roberts.senate.gov/public/?p=EmailPat

KENTUCKY

McConnell, Mitch - (R - KY)
317 Russell Senate Office Building Washington DC 20510
(202) 224-2541
Contact: www.mcconnell.senate.gov/public/index.cfm?p=contact

Paul, Rand - (R - KY)
167 Russell Senate Office Building Washington DC 20510
(202) 224-4343
Contact: www.paul.senate.gov/connect/email-rand

LOUISIANA

Cassidy, Bill - (R - LA)
520 Hart Senate Office Building Washington DC 20510 (202) 224-5824
Contact: www.cassidy.senate.gov/contact

Kennedy, John - (R - LA)
383 Russell Senate Office Building Washington DC 20510
(202) 224-4623
Contact: www.kennedy.senate.gov/content/contact-senator

MASSACHUSETTS

Markey, Edward J. - (D - MA)
255 Dirksen Senate Office Building Washington DC 20510
(202) 224-2742
Contact: www.markey.senate.gov/contact

Warren, Elizabeth - (D - MA)
317 Hart Senate Office Building Washington DC 20510
(202) 224-4543
Contact: www.warren.senate.gov/?p=email_senator

MARYLAND

Cardin, Benjamin L. - (D - MD)
509 Hart Senate Office Building Washington DC 20510
(202) 224-4524
Contact: www.cardin.senate.gov/contact/

MARYLAND cont.

Van Hollen, Chris - (D - MD)
110 Hart Senate Office Building Washington DC 20510
(202) 224-4654
Contact: www.vanhollen.senate.gov/content/contact-senator

MAINE

Collins, Susan M. - (R - ME)
413 Dirksen Senate Office Building Washington DC 20510
(202) 224-2523
Contact: www.collins.senate.gov/contact

King, Angus S., Jr. - (I - ME)
133 Hart Senate Office Building Washington DC 20510
(202) 224-5344
Contact: www.king.senate.gov/contact

MICHIGAN

Peters, Gary C. - (D - MI)
724 Hart Senate Office Building Washington DC 20510
202) 224-6221
Contact: www.peters.senate.gov/contact/email-gary

Stabenow, Debbie - (D - MI)
731 Hart Senate Office Building Washington DC 20510
(202) 224-4822
Contact: www.stabenow.senate.gov/contact

MINNESOTA

Franken, Al - (D - MN)
309 Hart Senate Office Building Washington DC 20510
(202) 224-5641
Contact: www.franken.senate.gov/?p=contact

Klobuchar, Amy - (D - MN)
302 Hart Senate Office Building Washington DC 20510
(202) 224-3244
Contact: www.klobuchar.senate.gov/public/index.cfm/contact

MISSOURI

Blunt, Roy - (R - MO)
260 Russell Senate Office Building Washington DC 20510
(202) 224-5721
Contact: www.blunt.senate.gov/public/index.cfm/contact-roy

McCaskill, Claire - (D - MO)
503 Hart Senate Office Building Washington DC 20510
(202) 224-6154
Contact: www.mccaskill.senate.gov/contact

MISSISSIPPI

Cochran, Thad - (R - MS)
113 Dirksen Senate Office Building Washington DC 20510
(202) 224-5054
Contact: www.cochran.senate.gov/public/index.cfm/email-me

Wicker, Roger F. - (R - MS)
555 Dirksen Senate Office Building Washington DC 20510
(202) 224-6253
Contact: www.wicker.senate.gov/public/index.cfm/contact

MONTANA

Daines, Steve - (R - MT)
320 Hart Senate Office Building Washington DC 20510
(202) 224-2651
Contact: www.daines.senate.gov/connect/email-steve

Tester, Jon - (D - MT)
311 Hart Senate Office Building Washington DC 20510
(202) 224-2644
Contact: www.tester.senate.gov/?p=email_senator

NORTH CAROLINA

Burr, Richard - (R - NC)
217 Russell Senate Office Building Washington DC 20510
(202) 224-3154
Contact: www.burr.senate.gov/contact/email

Tillis, Thom - (R - NC)
185 Dirksen Senate Office Building Washington DC 20510
(202) 224-6342
Contact: www.tillis.senate.gov/public/index.cfm/email-me

NORTH DAKOTA

Heitkamp, Heidi - (D - ND)
516 Hart Senate Office Building Washington DC 20510
(202) 224-2043
Contact: www.heitkamp.senate.gov/public/index.cfm/contact

NORTH DAKOTA cont.

Hoeven, John - (R - ND)
338 Russell Senate Office Building Washington DC 20510
(202) 224-2551
Contact: www.hoeven.senate.gov/public/index.cfm/email-the-senator

NEBRASKA

Fischer, Deb - (R - NE)
454 Russell Senate Office Building Washington DC 20510
(202) 224-6551
Contact: www.fischer.senate.gov/public/index.cfm/contact

Sasse, Ben - (R - NE)
136 Russell Senate Office Building Washington DC 20510
(202) 224-4224
Contact: www.sasse.senate.gov/public/index.cfm/email-ben

NEW HAMPSHIRE

Hassan, Margaret Wood - (D - NH)
330 Hart Senate Office Building Washington DC 20510
(202) 224-3324
Contact: www.hassan.senate.gov/content/contact-senator

Shaheen, Jeanne - (D - NH)
506 Hart Senate Office Building Washington DC 20510
(202) 224-2841
Contact: www.shaheen.senate.gov/contact/contact-jeanne

NEW JERSEY

Booker, Cory A. - (D - NJ)
359 Dirksen Senate Office Building Washington DC 20510
(202) 224-3224
Contact: www.booker.senate.gov/?p=contact

Menendez, Robert - (D - NJ)
528 Hart Senate Office Building Washington DC 20510
(202) 224-4744
Contact: www.menendez.senate.gov/contact

NEW MEXICO

Heinrich, Martin - (D - NM)
303 Hart Senate Office Building Washington DC 20510
(202) 224-5521
Contact: www.heinrich.senate.gov/contact

Udall, Tom - (D - NM)
531 Hart Senate Office Building Washington DC 20510
(202) 224-6621
Contact: www.tomudall.senate.gov/?p=contact

NEVADA

Cortez Masto, Catherine - (D - NV)
204 Russell Senate Office Building Washington DC 20510
(202) 224-3542
Contact: www.cortezmasto.senate.gov/content/contact-senator

Heller, Dean - (R - NV)
324 Hart Senate Office Building Washington DC 20510
(202) 224-6244
Contact: www.heller.senate.gov/public/index.cfm/contact-form

NEW YORK

Gillibrand, Kirsten E. - (D - NY)
478 Russell Senate Office Building Washington DC 20510
(202) 224-4451
Contact: www.gillibrand.senate.gov/contact/

Schumer, Charles E. - (D - NY)
322 Hart Senate Office Building Washington DC 20510
(202) 224-6542
Contact: www.schumer.senate.gov/contact/email-chuck

OHIO

Brown, Sherrod - (D - OH)
713 Hart Senate Office Building Washington DC 20510
(202) 224-2315
Contact: www.brown.senate.gov/contact/

Portman, Rob - (R - OH)
448 Russell Senate Office Building Washington DC 20510
(202) 224-3353
Contact: www.portman.senate.gov/public/index.cfm/contact?p=contact...

OKLAHOMA

Inhofe, James M. - (R - OK)
205 Russell Senate Office Building Washington DC 20510
(202) 224-4721
Contact: www.inhofe.senate.gov/contact

OKLAHOMA cont.

Lankford, James - (R - OK)
316 Hart Senate Office Building Washington DC 20510
(202) 224-5754
Contact: www.lankford.senate.gov/contact/email

OREGON

Merkley, Jeff - (D - OR)
313 Hart Senate Office Building Washington DC 20510
(202) 224-3753
Contact: www.merkley.senate.gov/contact/

Wyden, Ron - (D - OR)
221 Dirksen Senate Office Building Washington DC 20510 (
202) 224-5244
Contact: www.wyden.senate.gov/contact/

PENNSYLVANIA

Casey, Robert P., Jr. - (D - PA)
393 Russell Senate Office Building Washington DC 20510
(202) 224-6324
Contact: www.casey.senate.gov/contact/

Toomey, Patrick J. - (R - PA)
248 Russell Senate Office Building Washington DC 20510
(202) 224-4254
Contact: www.toomey.senate.gov/?p=contact

RHODE ISLAND

Reed, Jack - (D - RI)
728 Hart Senate Office Building Washington DC 20510
(202) 224-4642
Contact: www.reed.senate.gov/contact/

Whitehouse, Sheldon - (D - RI)
530 Hart Senate Office Building Washington DC 20510
(202) 224-2921
Contact: www.whitehouse.senate.gov/contact/email-sheldon

SOUTH CAROLINA

Graham, Lindsey - (R - SC)
290 Russell Senate Office Building Washington DC 20510
(202) 224-5972
Contact: www.lgraham.senate.gov/public/index.cfm/e-mail-senator-gr...

Scott, Tim - (R - SC)
717 Hart Senate Office Building Washington DC 20510
(202) 224-6121
Contact: www.scott.senate.gov/contact/email-me

SOUTH DAKOTA

Rounds, Mike - (R - SD)
502 Hart Senate Office Building Washington DC 20510
(202) 224-5842
Contact: www.rounds.senate.gov/contact/email-mike

Thune, John - (R - SD)
511 Dirksen Senate Office Building Washington DC 20510
(202) 224-2321
Contact: www.thune.senate.gov/public/index.cfm/contact

TENNESSEE

Alexander, Lamar - (R - TN)
455 Dirksen Senate Office Building Washington DC 20510
(202) 224-4944
Contact: www.alexander.senate.gov/public/index.cfm?p=Email

Corker, Bob - (R - TN)
425 Dirksen Senate Office Building Washington DC 20510
(202) 224-3344
Contact: www.corker.senate.gov/public/index.cfm/emailme

TEXAS

Cornyn, John - (R - TX)
517 Hart Senate Office Building Washington DC 20510
(202) 224-2934
Contact: www.cornyn.senate.gov/contact

Cruz, Ted - (R - TX)
404 Russell Senate Office Building Washington DC 20510
(202) 224-5922
Contact: www.cruz.senate.gov/?p=email_senator

UTAH

Hatch, Orrin G. - (R - UT)
104 Hart Senate Office Building Washington DC 20510
(202) 224-5251
Contact: www.hatch.senate.gov/public/index.cfm/contact?p=Email-Orrin

UTAH cont.

Lee, Mike - (R - UT)
361A Russell Senate Office Building Washington DC 20510
(202) 224-5444
Contact: www.lee.senate.gov/public/index.cfm/contact

VIRGINIA

Kaine, Tim - (D - VA)
231 Russell Senate Office Building Washington DC 20510
(202) 224-4024
Contact: www.kaine.senate.gov/contact

Warner, Mark R. - (D - VA)
703 Hart Senate Office Building Washington DC 20510
(202) 224-2023
Contact: www.warner.senate.gov/public/index.cfm?p=Contact

VERMONT

Leahy, Patrick J. - (D - VT)
437 Russell Senate Office Building Washington DC 20510
(202) 224-4242
Contact: www.leahy.senate.gov/contact/

Sanders, Bernard - (I - VT)
332 Dirksen Senate Office Building Washington DC 20510
(202) 224-5141
Contact: www.sanders.senate.gov/contact/

WASHINGTON

Cantwell, Maria - (D - WA)
511 Hart Senate Office Building Washington DC 20510
(202) 224-3441
Contact: www.cantwell.senate.gov/public/index.cfm/email-maria

Murray, Patty - (D - WA)
154 Russell Senate Office Building Washington DC 20510
(202) 224-2621
Contact: www.murray.senate.gov/public/index.cfm/contactme

WISCONSIN

Baldwin, Tammy - (D - WI)
709 Hart Washington DC 20510
(202) 224-5653
Contact: www.baldwin.senate.gov/feedback

Johnson, Ron - (R - WI)
328 Hart Senate Office Building Washington DC 20510
(202) 224-5323
Contact: www.ronjohnson.senate.gov/public/index.cfm/email-the-sena...

WEST VIRGINIA

Capito, Shelley Moore - (R - WV)
 172 Russell Senate Office Building Washington DC 20510
(202) 224-6472
Contact: www.capito.senate.gov/contact/contact-shelley

Manchin, Joe, III - (D - WV)
306 Hart Senate Office Building Washington DC 20510
(202) 224-3954
Contact: www.manchin.senate.gov/public/index.cfm/contact-form

WYOMING

Barrasso, John - (R - WY)
307 Dirksen Senate Office Building Washington DC 20510
(202) 224-6441
Contact: www.barrasso.senate.gov/public/index.cfm/contact-form

Enzi, Michael B. - (R - WY)
379A Russell Senate Office Building Washington DC 20510
(202) 224-3424
Contact: www.enzi.senate.gov/public/index.cfm/contact?p=e-mail-sen...

U. S. House of Representatives

Alabama

Rep. Jo Bonner (R-1st)
2236 Rayburn House Office Building
(202) 225-4931; 225-0562
Mobile: (334) 690-2811
Web Site

Rep. Martha Roby (R-2nd)
414 Cannon Office Building
(202) 225- 2901: 225-8913
Dothan: (334) 794-9680
Web Site

Rep. Michael Rogers (R-3rd)
324 Cannon House Office Building
(202) 225-3261; 226-8485
Anniston: (256) 236-5655
Web Site

Robert B. Aderholt (R-4th)
2264 Rayburn House Office Building
(202) 225-4876; 225-5587
Jasper: (205) 221-2310
Web Site

Rep. Mo Brooks (R-5th)
1641 Longworth House Office Building
(202) 225-4801; 225-4392
Huntsville: (256) 551-0190
Web Site

Rep. Spencer Bachus (R-6th)
2246 Rayburn House Office Building
(202) 225-4921; 226-2082
Birmingham: (205) 969-2296
Web Site

Rep. Terri Sewell (D-7th)
1133 Longworth House Office Building
(202) 225-2665; 226-9567
Birmingham: (205) 254-1960
Web Site

Alaska

Rep. Don Young (R-AL)
2314 Rayburn House Office Building
(202)225-5765; 225-0425
Anchorage: (907) 271-5978
Web Site

Amer'n Samoa

Del. Eni Faleomavaega (D-AL)
2422 Rayburn House Office Building
(202) 225-8577; 225-8757
Pago Pago: (684) 633-1372
Web Site

Arizona

Rep. Ann Kirkpatrick (D-1st) **
330 Cannon House Office Building
(202) 225-3361; 225-9739
Casa Grande: (520) 316-0839
Web Site

Rep. Ron Barber (D-2nd) **
1029 Longworth House Office Building
(202) 225-2542; 225-0378
Sierra Vista: (520) 459-3115
Web Site

Rep. Raul M. Grijalva (D-3rd)
1511 Longworth House Office Building
(202) 225-2435; 225-1541
Tucson: (520) 622-6788
Web Site

Rep. Paul Gosar (R-4th) **
504 Cannon House Office Building
(202) 225-2315; 225-9739
Prescott: (928) 445-1683
Web Site

Arizona cont.

Rep. Matt Salmon (R-5th) **
2349 Rayburn House Office Building
(202) 225-2635: 226-4386
Gilbert: (480) 699-8239

Rep. David Schweikert (R-6th)
1205 Longworth House Office Building
(202) 225-2190; 225-0096
Scottsdale: (480) 946-2411
Web Site

Rep. Ed Pastor (D-7th)
2465 Rayburn House Office Building
(202) 225-4065; 225-1655
Phoenix: (928) 256-0551
Web Site

Rep. Trent Franks (R-8th)
2435 Rayburn House Office Building
(202) 225-4576; 225-6328
Glendale: (623) 776-7911
Web Site

Rep. Kyrsten Sinema (D-9th) **
1237 Longworth House Office Building
(202) 225-9888; N/A
Phoenix: N/A
Web Site

Arkansas

Rep. Rick Crawford (R-1st)
1408 Longworth House Office Building
(202) 225-4076; 225-5602
Jonesboro: (870) 972-4600
Web Site

Rep. Tim Griffin (R-2nd)
1232 Longworth House Office Building
(202) 225-2506; 225-5903
Little Rock: (501) 324-5941
Web Site

Rep. Steve Womack (R-3rd)
1508 Longworth House Office Building
(202) 225-4301; 225-5713
Fort Smith: (479) 424-1146

Arkansas cont.

Rep. Tom Cotton (R-4th) **
415 Cannon House Office Building
(202) 225-3772; 225-1314
Pine Bluff: (870) 536-3376
Web Site

California

Rep. Doug LaMalfa (R-1st) **
506 Cannon House Office Building
(202) 225-3076; 226-0852
Oroville: N/A

Rep. Jared Huffman (D-2nd) **
1630 Longworth House Office Building
(202) 225-5161; N/A
Eureka: (707) 407-3585
Web Site

Rep. John Garamendi (D-3rd)
2438 Rayburn House Office Building
(202) 225-1880 ; 225-5914
Fairfield: (707) 438-1822
Web Site

Rep. Tom McClintock (R-4th)
428 Cannon House Office Building
(202) 225-2511; 225-5444
Granite Bay: (916) 786-5560
Web Site

Rep. Mike Thompson (D-5th)
231 Cannon House Office Building
(202) 225-3311; 225-4335
Napa: (707) 226-9898
Web Site

Rep. Doris Matsui (D-6th)
222 Cannon House Office Building
(202) 225-7163; 225-0566
Sacramento: (916) 498-5600
Web Site

Rep. Ami B. Bera (D-7th) **
1408 Longworth House Office Building
(202) 225-5716; 226-1298
N/A

California cont.

Rep. Paul Cook (R-8th) **
1222 Longworth House Office Building
(202) 225-5861; 225-6498
Apple Valley: N/A
Web Site

Rep. Jerry McNerney (D-9th)
1210 Longworth House Office Building
(202) 225-1947; 225-4060
Pleasanton: (925) 737-0727
Web Site

Rep. Jeff Denham (R-10th)
1730 Longworth House Office Building
(202) 225-4540; 225-3402
Modesto: (209) 579-5458
Web Site

Rep. George Miller (D-11th)
2205 Rayburn House Office Building
(202) 225-2095; 225-5609
Concord: (925) 602-1880
Web Site

Rep. Nancy Pelosi (D-12th)
235 Cannon House Office Building
(202) 225-4965; 225-8259
San Francisco: (415) 556-4862
Web Site

Rep. Barbara Lee (D-13th)
2267 Rayburn House Office Building
(202) 225-2661; 225-9817
Oakland: (510) 763-0370
Web Site

Rep. Jackie Speier (D-14th)
211 Cannon House Office Building
(202) 225-3531; 226-4183
San Mateo: (650) 342-0300
Web Site

Rep. Eric Swalwell (D-15th) **
501 Cannon House Office Building
(202) 225-5065; 226-3805
N/A
Web Site

California cont.

Rep. Jim Costa (D-16th)
1314 Longworth House Office Building
(202) 225-3341; 225-9308
Fresno: (559) 495-1620
Web Site

Rep. Mike Honda (D-17th)
1713 Longworth House Office Building
(202) 225-2631; 225-2699
Campbell: (408) 558-8085
Web Site

Rep. Anna Eshoo (D-18th)
205 Cannon House Office Building
(202) 225-8104; 225-8890
Palo Alto: (650) 323-2984
Web Site

Rep. Zoe Lofgren (D-19th)
1401 Longworth House Office Building
(202) 225-3072; 225-3336
San Jose: (408) 271-8700
Web Site

Rep. Sam Farr (D-20th)
1126 Longworth House Office Building
(202) 225-2861; 225-6791
Salinas: (831) 424-2229
Web Site

Rep. David Valadao (R-21st) **
1004 Longworth House Office Building
(202) 225-4695; 225-3196
Hanford: N/A
Web Site

Rep. Devin Nunes (R-22nd)
1013 Longworth House Office Building
(202) 225-2523; 225-3404
Visalia: (559) 733-3861
Web Site

Rep. Kevin McCarthy (R-23rd)
326 Cannon House Office Building
(202) 225-2915; 225-2908
Bakersfield: (661) 327-3611
Web Site

California cont.

Rep. Lois Capps (D-24th)
2231 Rayburn House Office Building
(202) 225-3601; 225-5632
Santa Barbara: (805) 730-1710
Web Site

Rep. Buck McKeon (R-25th)
2184 Rayburn House Office Building
(202) 225-1956; 226-0683
Santa Clarita: (805) 254-2111
Web Site

Rep. Julia Brownley (D-26th) **
1019 Longworth House Office Building
(202) 225-5811; 225-7018
N/A
Web Site

Rep. Judy Chu (D-27th)
1520 Longworth House Office Building
(202) 225-5464; 225-5467
El Monte: (626) 448-1271
Web Site

Rep. Adam Schiff (D-28th)
2411 Rayburn House Office Building
(202) 225-4176; 225-5828
Pasadena: (626) 304-2727
Web Site

Rep. Tony Cardenas (D-29th) **
1508 Longworth House Office Building
(202) 225-6131; 225-0819
N/A
Web Site

Rep. Brad Sherman (D-30th)
2242 Rayburn House Office Building
(202) 225-5911; 225-5879
Van Nuys: (818) 501-9200
Web Site

Rep. Gary Miller (R-31st)
2349 Rayburn House Office Building
(202) 225-3201; 226-6962
Brea: (714) 257-1142
Web Site

California cont.

Rep. Grace Napolitano (D-32nd)
1610 Longworth House Office Building
(202) 225-5256; 225-0027
Santa Fe Springs: (801) 801-2134
Web Site

Rep. Henry Waxman (D-33rd)
2204 Rayburn House Office Building
(202) 225-3976; 225-4099
Los Angeles: (323) 651-1040
Web Site

Rep. Xavier Becerra (D-34th)
1226 Longworth House Office Building
(202) 225-6235; 225-2202
Los Angeles: (213) 483-1425
Web Site

Rep. Gloria McLeod (D-35th) **
1641 Longworth House Office Building
(202) 225-6161; 225-8671
Montclair: (909) 626-2054
Web Site

Rep. Raul Ruiz (D-36th) **
1319 Longworth House Office Building
(202) 225-5330; 225-2961
Palm Springs: N/A
Web Site

Rep. Karen Bass (D-37th)
408 Cannon House Office Building
(202) 225-7084; 225-2422
Los Angeles: (323) 965-1422
Web Site

Rep. Linda Sanchez (D-38th)
2423 Rayburn House Office Building
(202) 225-6676; 226-1012
Cerritos: (562) 860-5050
Web Site

Rep. Ed Royce (R-39th)
2185 Rayburn House Office Building
(202) 225-4111; 226-0335
Orange: (714) 744-4130
Web Site

California cont.

Rep. Lucille Roybal-Allard (D-40th)
2330 Rayburn House Office Building
(202) 225-1766; 226-0350
Los Angeles: (213) 628-9230
Web Site

Rep. Mark Takano (D-41st) **
1507 Longworth House Office Building
(202) 225-2305; 225-7018
Riverside: N/A
Web Site

Rep. Ken Calvert (R-42nd)
2269 Rayburn House Office Building
(202) 225-1986; 225-2004
Riverside: (909) 784-4300
Web Site

Rep. Maxine Waters (D-43rd)
2344 Rayburn House Office Building
(202) 225-2201; 225-7854
Los Angeles: (213) 757-8900
Web Site

Rep. Janice Hahn (D-44th)
2400 Rayburn House Office Building
(202) 225-8220; 225-7290
Wilmington: (310) 549-8282
Web Site

Rep. John Campbell (R-45th)
1507 Longworth House Office Building
(202) 225-5611; 225-9177
Newport Beach: (949) 756-2244
Web Site

Rep. Loretta Sanchez (D-46th)
1114 Longworth House Office Building
(202) 225-2965; 225-5859
Garden Grove: (714) 621-0102
Web Site

Rep. Alan Lowenthal (D-47th) **
515 Cannon House Office Building
(202) 225-7924; 225-7926
Long Beach: (562) 436-3828
Web Site

California cont.

Rep. Dana Rohrabacher (R-48th)
2300 Rayburn House Office Building
(202) 225-2415; 225-0145
Huntington Beach: (714) 960-6483
Web Site

Rep. Darrell Issa (R-49th)
2347 Rayburn House Office Building
(202) 225-3906; 225-3303
Vista: (760) 599-5000
Web Site

Rep. Duncan Hunter (R-50th)
223 Cannon House Office Building
(202) 225-5672; 225-0235
El Cajon: (619) 448-5201
Web Site

Rep. Juan Vargas (D-51st) **
1605 Longworth House Office Building
(202) 225-8045; 225-9073
Chula Vista: (619) 422-5963
Web Site

Rep. Scott Peters (D-52nd) **
2410 Rayburn House Office Building
(202) 225-0508; 225-2558
N/A
Web Site

Rep. Susan Davis (D-53rd)
1526 Longworth House Office Building
(202) 225-2040; 225-2948
San Diego: (619) 280-5353
Web Site

Colorado

Rep. Diana DeGette (D-1st)
2335 Rayburn House Office Building
(202) 225-4431; 225-5657
Denver: (303) 844-4988
Web Site

Colorado cont.

Rep. Jared Polis (D-2nd)
501 Cannon House Office Building
(202) 225-2161; 226-7840
Boulder: (303) 484-9596
Web Site

Rep. Scott Tipton (R-3rd)
218 Cannon House Office Building
(202) 225-4761; 226-9669
Grand Junction: (970) 241-2499
Web Site

Rep. Cory Gardner (R-4th)
213 Cannon House Office Building
(202) 225-4676; 225-5870
Ft. Collins: (970) 221-7110
Web Site

Rep. Doug Lamborn (R-5th)
437 Cannon House Office Building
(202) 225-4422; 226-2638
Colorado Springs: (719) 520-0055
Web Site

Rep. Mike Coffman (R-6th)
1222 Longworth House Office Building
(202) 225-7882; 226-4623
Long Tree: (720) 283-9772
Web Site

Rep. Ed Perlmutter (D-7th)
1221 Longworth House Office Building
(202) 225-2645; 225-5278
Lakewood: (303) 274-7944
Web Site

Connecticut

Rep. John Larson (D-1st)
1501 Longworth House Office Building
(202) 225-2265; 225-1031
Hartford: (860) 278-8888

Conneticut cont.

Rep. Joseph Courtney (D-2nd)
215 Cannon House Office Building
(202) 225-2076; 225-4977
Norwich: (860) 886-0139
Web Site

Rep. Rosa DeLauro (D-3rd)
2413 Rayburn House Office Building
(202) 225-3661; 225-4890
New Haven: (203) 562-3718
Web Site

Rep. Jim Himes (D-4th)
119 Cannon House Office Building
(202) 225-5541; 225-9629
Bridgeport: (866) 453-0028
Web Site

Rep. Elizabeth Esty (D-5th) **
509 Cannon House Office Building
(202) 225-4476; 225-5933
New Britain: N/A
Web Site

Delaware

Rep. John Carney (D-AL)
1406 Longworth House Office Building
(202) 225-4165; 225-2291
Wilmington: (302) 691-7333
Web Site

District of Columbia

Del. Eleanor Holmes Norton (D-AL)
2136 Rayburn House Office Building
(202) 225-8050; 225-3002
Washington: (202) 783-5065
Web Site

Florida

Rep. Jeff Miller (R-1st)
336 Cannon House Office Building
(202) 225-4136; 225-3414
Pensacola: (850) 479-1183
Web Site

Rep. Steve Southerland (R-2nd)
1229 Longworth House Office Building
(202) 225-5235; 225-5615
Panama City: (850) 785-0812
Web Site

Rep. Tedd Yoho (R-3rd) **
511 Cannon House Office Building
(202) 225-5744; 225-2256
Gainsville: N/A
Web Site

Rep. Ander Crenshaw (R-4th)
440 Cannon House Office Building
(202) 225-2501; 225-2504
Jacksonville: (904) 598-0481
Web Site

Rep. Corrine Brown (D-5th)
2111 Rayburn House Office Building
(202) 225-0123; 225-2256
Jacksonville: (904) 354-1652
Web Site

Rep. Ron DeSantis (R-6th) **
427 Cannon House Office Building
(202) 225-2706; 225-3973
Port Orange: (386) 756-9798
Web Site

Rep. John Mica (R-7th)
2187 Rayburn House Office Building
(202) 225-4035; 226-0821
Maitland: (407) 657-8080
Web Site

Rep. Bill Posey (R-8th)
120 Cannon House Office Building
(202) 225-3671; 225-3516
Melbourne: (407) 632-1776
Web Site

Florida cont.

Rep. Alan Grayson (D-9th) **
430 Cannon House Office Building
(202) 225-9889; 225-4085
Palm Harbor?: N/A
Web Site

Rep. Daniel Webster (R-10th)
1039 Longworth House Office Building
(202) 225-2176; 225-0999
Winter Garden: (407) 654-5705
Web Site

Rep. Richard Nugent (R-11th)
1727 Longworth House Office Building
(202) 225-1002; 226-6559
Brooksville: (352) 799-8354
Web Site

Rep. Gus M. Bilirakis (R-12th)
2313 Rayburn House Office Building
(202) 225-5755; 225-4085
Tarpon Springs: (727) 940-5860

Rep. Bill Young (R-13th)
2407 Rayburn House Office Building
(202) 225-5961; 225-9764
St. Petersburg: (813) 893-3191
Web Site

Rep. Kathy Castor (D-14th)
205 Cannon House Office Building
(202) 225-3376; 225-5652
Tampa: (813) 871-2817
Web Site

Rep. Dennis Ross (R-15th)
229 Cannon House Offcie Building
(202) 225-1252; 226-0585
Lakeland: (863) 644-8215
Web Site

Rep. Vern Buchanan (R-16th)
2104 Rayburn House Office Building
(202) 225-5015; 226-0828
Sarasota: (941) 951-6643
Web Site

Florida cont.

Rep. Tom Rooney (R-17th)
221 Cannon House Office Building
(202) 225-5792; 225-3132
Punta Gorda: (941) 575-9101
Web Site

Rep. Patrick Murphy (D-18th) **
1517 Longworth House Office Building
(202) 225-3026; 225-8398
Palm Beach Gardens: (561) 253-8433
Web Site

Rep. Trey Radel (R-19th) **
1123 Longworth House Office Building
(202) 225-2536; 225-5974
Cape Coral: N/A
Web Site

Rep. Alcee Hastings (D-20th)
2353 Rayburn House Office Building
(202) 225-1313; 225-1171
Ft. Lauderdale: (954) 733-2800
Web Site

Rep. Ted Deutch (R-21st)
1024 Longworth House Office Building
(202) 225-3001; 225-5974
Boca Raton: (561) 470-5440
Web Site

Rep. Lois Frankel (D-22nd) **
1037 Longworth House Office Building
(202) 225-9890; 225-8398
Boca Raton: (561) 998-9045
Web Site

Rep. Debbie Wasserman Schultz (D-23)
118 Cannon House Office Building
(202) 225-7931; 226-2052
Pembroke Pines: (954) 437-3936
Web Site

Rep. Frederica Wilson (D-24th)
208 Cannon House Offcie Building
(202) 225-4506; 226-0777
Miami Gardens: (305) 690-5905
Web Site

Florida cont.

Rep. Mario Diaz-Balart (R-25th)
436 Cannon House Office Building
(202) 225-4211; 225-8576
Miami: (305) 225-6866
Web Site

Rep. Joe Garcia (D-26th) **
1440 Cannon House Office Building
(202) 225-2778; 226-0346
Miami: N/A
Web Site

Rep. Ileana Ros-Lehtinen (R-27th)
2206 Rayburn House Office Building
(202) 225-3931; 225-5620
Miami: (305) 668-2285
Web Site

Georgia

Rep. Jack Kingston (R-1st)
2372 Rayburn House Office Building
(202) 225-5831; 226-2269
Savannah: (912) 352-0101
Web Site

Rep. Sanford Bishop, Jr. (D-2nd)
2429 Rayburn House Office Building
(202) 225-3631; 225-2203
Albany: (912) 439-8067
Web Site

Rep. Lynn Westmoreland (R-3rd)
2433 Rayburn House Office Building
(202) 225-5901; 225-2515
Newnan: (770) 683-2033
Web Site

Rep. Hank Johnson (D-4th)
1427 Longworth House Office Building
(202) 225-1605; 226-0691
Lithonia: (770) 987-2291
Web Site

Rep. John Lewis (D-5th)
343 Cannon House Office Building
(202) 225-3801; 225-0351
Atlanta: (404) 659-0116

Georgia cont.

Rep. Tom Price (R-6th)
403 Cannon House Office Building
(202) 225-4501; 225-4656
Marietta: (770) 565-4990
Web Site

Rep. Rob Woodall (R-7th)
1725 Longworth House Office Building
(202) 225-4272; 225-4696
Lawrenceville: (770) 232-3005
Web Site

Rep. Austin Scott (D-8th)
516 Cannon House Office Building
(202) 225-6531; 225-3013
Warner Robins: (478) 971-1776
Web Site

Rep. Doug Collins (R-9th) **
513 Cannon House Office Building
(202) 225-9893; N/A
Gainsville: N/A
Web Site

Rep. Paul Broun (R-10th)
325 Cannon House Office Building
(202) 225-4101; 226-0776
Evans: (706) 447-3857
Web Site

Rep. Phil Gingrey (R-11th)
442 Cannon House Office Building
(202) 225-2931; 225-2944
Marietta: (770) 429-1776
Web Site

Rep. John Barrow (D-12th)
2202 Rayburn House Office Building
(202) 225-2823; 225-3377
Augusta: (706) 722-4494
Web Site

Rep. David Scott (D-13th)
225 Cannon House Office Building
(202) 225-2939; 225-4628
Jonesboro: (770) 210-5073
Web Site

Georgia cont.

Rep. Tom Graves (R-14th)
1113 Longworth House Office Building
(202) 225-5211; 225-8272
Dalton: 706-226-5320
Web Site

Guam

Del. Madeleine Bordallo (D-AL)
2441 Rayburn House Office Building
(202) 225-1118; 226-0341
Hagatna: (671) 477-4272
Web Site

Hawaii

Rep. Colleen Hanabusa (D-1st)
238 Cannon House Office Building
(202) 225-2726; 225-4580
Honolulu: (808) 541-2570
Web Site

Rep. Tulsi Gabbard (D-2nd) **
502 Cannon House Office Building
(202) 225-4906; 225-4987
Honolulu: N/A
Web Site

Idaho

Rep. Raul Labrador (R-1st)
1523 Longworth House Office Building
(202) 225-6611; 225-3029
Meridan: (208) 888-3188
Web Site

Rep. Mike Simpson (R-2nd)
2312 Rayburn House Office Building
(202) 225-5531; 225-8216
Boise: (208) 334-1953
Web Site

Illinois

Rep. Bobby Rush (D-1st)
2268 Rayburn House Office Building
(202) 225-4372; 226-0333
Chicago: (773) 224-6500
Web Site

Rep. VACANT (-2nd) **
Special Election April 9, 2013
2419 Rayburn House Office Building
(202) 225-0773; 225-0899
Chicago: (773) 734-9660
Web Site

Rep. Dan Lipinski (D-3rd)
1717 Longworth House Office Building
(202) 225-5701; 225-1012
Chicago: (312) 886-0481
Web Site

Rep. Luiz Gutierrez (D-4th)
2266 Rayburn House Office Building
(202) 225-8203; 225-7810
Chicago: (773) 342-0774
Web Site

Rep. Mike Quigley (D-5th)
1124 Longworth House Office Building
(202) 225-4061; 225-5603
Chicago: (773) 267-5926
Web Site

Rep. Peter Roskam (R-6th)
227 Cannon House Office Building
(202) 225-4561; 225-1166
Bloomingdale: (630) 893-9670
Web Site

Rep. Danny Davis (D-7th)
2159 Rayburn House Office Building
(202) 225-5006; 225-5641
Chicago: (773) 533-7520
Web Site

Rep. Tammy Duckworth (D-8th) **
108 Cannon House Office Building
(202) 225-3711; 225-7830
Schaumburg: N/A
Web Site

Illinois cont.

Rep. Jan Schakowsky (D-9th)
2367 Rayburn House Office Building
(202) 225-2111; 226-6890
Chicago: (773) 506-7100
Web Site

Rep. Brad Schneider (D-10th) **
317 Cannon House Office Building
(202) 225-4835; 225-0837
Lincolnshire: (847) 793-0625
Web Site

Rep. Bill Foster (D-11th) **
2113 Rayburn House Office Building
(202) 225-3515; 225-9420
N/A
Web Site

Rep. William Enyart (D-12th) **
1722 Longworth House Office Building
(202) 225-5661; 225-0285
Belleville: (618) 233-8026
Web Site

Rep. Rodney Davis (R-13th) **
1740 Longworth House Office Building
(202) 225-2371; 226-0791
Champaign: (217) 403-4690
Web Site

Rep. Randy Hultgren (R-14th)
332 Cannon House Office Building
(202) 225-2976; 225-0697
Geneva: (630) 232-7104
Web Site

Rep. John Shimkus (R-15th)
2452 Rayburn House Office Building
(202) 225-5271; 225-5880
Springfield: (217) 492-5090
Web Site

Rep. Adam Kinzinger (R-16th)
1221 Longworth House Office Building
(202) 225-3635; 225-3521
Joliet: (815) 726-4998
Web Site

Illinois cont.

Rep. Cheri Bustos (D-17th) **
1009 Longworth House Office Building
(202) 225-5905; 225-5396
Rock Island: (309) 786-3406
Web Site

Rep. Aaron Schock (R-18th)
328 Cannon House Office Building
(202) 225-6201; 225-9249
Peoria: (309) 671-7027
Web Site

Indiana

Rep. Peter Visclosky (D-1st)
2256 Rayburn House Office Building
(202) 225-2461; 225-2493
Merrillville: (219) 795-1844
Web Site

Rep. Jackie Walorski (R-2nd) **
419 Cannon House Office Building
(202) 225-3915; 225-6798
Mishawaka: (574) 204-2645
Web Site

Rep. Marlin Stutzman (R-3rd)
1728 Longworth House Office Building
(202) 225-4436; 226-9870
Winona Lake: (574) 269-1940
Web Site

Rep. Todd Rokita (R-4th)
236 Cannon House Office Building
(202) 225-5037;226-0544
Plainfield: (317) 838-0404
Web Site

Rep. Susan Brooks (R-5th) **
1505 Longworth House Office Building
(202) 225-2276; 225-0016
Indianapolis: (317) 848-0201

Indiana cont.

Rep. Luke Messer (R-6th) **
508 Cannon House Office Building
(202) 225-3021; 225-3382
Muncie: (765) 747-5566
Web Site

Rep. Andre Carson (D-7th)
425 Cannon House Office Building
(202) 225-4011; 225-5633
Indianapolis: (317) 283-6516
Web Site

Rep. Larry Bucshon (R-8th)
1123 Longworth House Office Building
(202) 225-4636; 225-3284
Evansville: (812) 465-6484
Web Site

Rep. Todd Young (R-9th)
1721 Longworth House Office Building
(202) 225-5315; 226-6866
Jeffersonville: (812) 288-3999
Web Site

Iowa

Rep. Bruce Braley (D-1st)
1727 Longworth House Office Building
(202) 225-2911; 225-6666
Waterloo: (319) 287-3233
Web Site

Rep. Dave Loebsack (D-2nd)
1527 Longworth House Office Building
(202) 225-6576; 226-0757
Iowa City: (319) 351-0789
Web Site

Rep. Tom Latham (R-3rd)
2217 Rayburn House Office Building
(202) 225-5476; 225-3301
Ames: (515) 232-2885
Web Site

Iowa cont.

Rep. Steve King (R-4th)
1131 Longworth House Office Building
(202) 225-4426; 225-3193
Storm Lake: (712) 732-4197
Web Site

Kansas

Rep. Tim Huelskamp (R-1st)
126 Cannon House Office Building
(202) 225-2715; 225-5124
Hutchinson: (620) 665-6138
Web Site

Rep. Lynn Jenkins (R-2nd)
1122 Longworth House Office Building
(202) 225-6601; 225-7986
Topeka: (785) 234-5966
Web Site

Rep. Kevin Yoder (R-3rd)
214 Cannon House Office Building
(202) 225-2865; 225-2807
Kansas City: (913) 621-0832
Web Site

Rep. Mike Pompeo (R-4th)
107 Cannon House Office Building
(202) 225-6216; 225-3489
Wichita: (316) 262-8992
Web Site

Kentucky

Rep. Edward Whitfield (R-1st)
2368 Rayburn House Office Building
(202) 225-3115; 225-3547
Hopkinsville: (502) 885-8079
Web Site

Rep. Brett Guthrie (R-2nd)
308 Cannon House Office Building
(202) 225-3501; 226-2019
Bowling Green: (270) 842-9896
Web Site

Kansas cont.

Rep. John Yarmuth (D-3rd)
435 Cannon House Office Building
(202) 225-5401; 225-5776
Louisville: (502) 582-5129
Web Site

Rep. Thomas Massie (R-4th) **
314 Cannon House Office Building
(202) 225-3465; 225-0003
Ft. Mitchell: (859) 426-0080
Web Site

Rep. Harold Rogers (R-5th)
2406 Rayburn House Office Building
(202) 225-4601; 225-0940
Somerset: (606) 679-8346
Web Site

Rep. Garland Barr, IV (R-6th) **
1432 Longworth House Office Building
(202) 225-4706; 225-2122
Lexington: (859) 219-1366
Web Site

Louisiana

Rep. Steve Scalise (R-1st)
429 Cannon House Office Building
Metairie: (504) 837-1259
Web Site

Rep. Cedric Richmond (D-2nd)
415 Cannon House Office Building
(202) 225-6636; 225-1988
New Orleans: (504) 288-3777
Web Site

Rep. Charles Boustany, Jr. (R-3rd)
1431 Longworth House Office Building
(202) 225-2031; 225-5724
Lafayette: (337) 235-6322
Web Site

Louisiana cont.

Rep. John Fleming (R-4th)
416 Cannon House Office Building
(202) 225-2777; 225-8039
Shreveport: (318) 798-2254
Web Site

Rep. Rodney Alexander (D-5th)
316 Cannon House Office Building
(202) 225-8490; 225-5639
Alexandria: (318) 445-0818
Web Site

Rep. Bill Cassidy (R-6th)
1535 Longworth House Office Building
(202) 225-3901; 225-7313
Baton Rouge: (504) 929-7711
Web Site

Maine

Rep. Chellie Pingree (D-1st)
1318 Longworth House Office Building
(202) 225-6116; 225-5590
Portland: (207) 774-5019
Web Site

Rep. Michael Michaud (D-2nd)
1724 Longworth House Office Building
(202) 225-6306; 225-2943
Bangor: (207) 942-6935
Web Site

Maryland

Rep. Andy Harris (R-1st)
506 Cannon House Office Building
(202) 225-5311; 225-0254
Salisbury: (443) 944-8624
Web Site

Rep. Dutch Ruppersberger (D-2nd)
2453 Rayburn House Office Building
(202) 225-3061; 225-3094
Timonium: (410) 628-2701
Web Site

Maryland cont.

Rep. John Sarbanes (D-3rd)
2444 Rayburn House Office Building
(202) 225-4016; 225-9219
Towson: (410) 832-8890
Web Site

Rep. Donna Edwards (D-4th)
318 Cannon House Office Building
(202) 225-8699; 225-8714
Silver Spring: (301) 562-7960
Web Site

Rep. Steny Hoyer (D-5th)
1705 Longworth House Office Building
(202) 225-4131; 225-4300
Greenbelt: (301) 474-0119
Web Site

Rep. John Delaney (D-6th) **
1632 Longworth House Office Building
(202) 225-2721; 225-2193
Gaithersburg: (301) 926-0300
Web Site

Rep. Elijah Cummings (D-7th)
2235 Rayburn House Office Building
(202) 225-4741; 225-3178
Baltimore: (410) 685-9199
Web Site

Rep. Chris Van Hollen, Jr. (D-8th)
1707 Longworth House Office Building
(202) 225-5341; 225-0375
Rockville: (301) 424-3501
Web Site

Massachusetts

Rep. Richard Neal (D-1st)
2208 Rayburn House Office Building
(202) 225-5601; 225-8112
Springfield: (413) 785-0325
Web Site

Massachusetts cont.

Rep. James McGovern (D-2nd)
4380 Cannon House Office Building
(202) 225-6101; 225-5759
Worcester: (508) 831-7356
Web Site

Rep. Niki Tsongas (D-3rd)
1607 Longworth House Office Building
(202) 225-3411; 226-0771
Lowell: (978) 459-0101
Web Site

Rep. Joseph P. Kennedy, III (D-4th) **
1218 Longworth House Office Building
(202) 225-5931; 225-0182
Newton: (617) 332-3333
Web Site

Rep. Edward Markey (D-5th)
2108 Rayburn House Office Building
(202) 225-2836; 226-0092
Medford: (781) 396-2900
Web Site

Rep. John Tierney (D-6th)
2238 Rayburn House Office Building
(202) 225-8020; 225-5915
Peabody: (978) 531-1669
Web Site

Rep. Michael Capuano (D-7th)
1414 Longworth House Office Building
(202) 225-5111; 225-9322
Cambridge: (617) 621-6208
Web Site

Rep. Stephen Lynch (D-8th)
2348 Rayburn House Office Building
(202) 225-8273; 225-3984
Boston: (617) 428-2000
Web Site

Rep. Bill Keating (D-9th)
315 Cannon House Office Building
(202) 225-3111; 225-5658
Quincy: (617) 770-3700
Web Site

Michigan

Rep. Dan Benishek (R-1st)
514 Cannon House Office Building
(202) 225-4735; 225-4710
Marquette: 906-273-1661
Web Site

Rep. Bill Huizenga (R-2nd)
1217 Longworth House Office Building
(202) 225-4401; 226-0779
Holland: (616) 395-0030
Web Site

Rep. Justin Amash (R-3rd)
114 Cannon House Office Building
(202) 225-3831; 225-5144
Grand Rapids: (616) 451-8383
Web Site

Rep. Dave Camp (R-4th)
341 Cannon House Office Building
(202) 225-3561; 225-9679
Midland: (989) 631-2552
Web Site

Rep. Dale Kildee (D-5th)
2107 Rayburn House Office Building
(202) 225-3611; 225-6393
Flint: (810) 239-1437
Web Site

Rep. Fred Upton (R-6th)
2183 Rayburn House Office Building
(202) 225-3761; 225-4986
Kalamazoo: (616) 385-0039
Web Site

Rep. Tim Walberg (R-7th)
418 Cannon House Office Building
(202) 225-6276; 225-6281
Jackson: (517) 780-9075
Web Site

Rep. Mike Rogers (R-8th)
133 Cannon House Office Building
(202) 225-4872; 225-5820
Lansing: (877) 333-6453
Web Site

Michigan cont.

Rep. Sandy Levin (D-9th)
1236 Longworth House Office Building
(202) 225-4961; 226-1033
Roseville: (586) 498-7122
Web Site

Rep. Candice Miller (R-10th)
1034 Longworth House Office Building
(202) 225-2106; 226-1169
Shelby Township: (586) 997-5010
Web Site

Rep. Kerry Bentivolio (R-11th) **
226 Cannon House Office Building
(202) 225-8171; 225-2667
Commerce: (248) 859-2982
Web Site

Rep. John Dingell (D-12th)
2328 Rayburn House Office Building
(202) 225-4071; 226-0371
Dearborn: (313) 278-2936
Web Site

Rep. John Conyers (D-13th)
2426 Rayburn House Office Building
(202) 225-5126; 225-0072
Detroit: (313) 961-5670
Web Site

Rep. Gary Peters (D-14th)
1609 Longworth House Office Building
(202) 225-5802; 226-2356
Troy: (248) 273-4227

Minnesota

Rep. Tim Walz (D-1st)
1722 Longworth House Office Building
(202) 225-2472; 225-3433
Mankato: (507) 388-2149
Web Site

Rep. John Kline (R-2nd)
2439 Rayburn House Office Building
(202) 225-2271; 225-2595
Burnsville: (952) 808-1213

Minnesota cont.

Rep. Erik Paulsen (R-3rd)
127 Cannon House Office Building
(202) 225-2871; 225-6351
Minnetonka: (952) 405-8510
Web Site

Rep. Betty McCollum (D-4th)
1714 Longworth House Office Building
(202) 225-6631; 225-1968
St. Paul: (612) 224-9191
Web Site

Rep. Keith Ellison (D-5th)
1027 Longworth House Office Building
(202) 225-4755; 225-4886
Minneapolis: (612) 522-1212
Web Site

Rep. Michele Bachmann (R-6th)
103 Cannon House Office Building
(202) 225-2331; 225-6475
Woodbury: (651) 731-5400
Web Site

Rep. Collin Peterson (D-7th)
2211 Rayburn House Office Building
(202) 225-2165; 225-1593
Detroit Lakes: (218) 847-5056
Web Site

Rep. Rick Nolan (D-8th) **
2447 Rayburn House Office Building
(202) 225-6211; 225-0699
Brainerd: (218) 545-4078
Web Site

Mississippi

Rep. Alan Nunnelee (R-1st)
1432 Longworth House Office Building
(202) 225-4306; 225-3549
Tupelo: (662) 841-8808

Mississippi cont.

Rep. Bennie Thompson (D-2nd)
2466 Rayburn House Office Building
(202) 225-5876; 225-5898
Bolton: (800) 355-9003
Web Site

Rep. Gregg Harper (R-3rd)
307 Cannon House Office Building
(202) 225-5031; 225-5797
Pearl: (601) 932-2410
Web Site

Rep. Steven Palazzo (R-4th)
331 Cannon House Office Building
(202) 225-5772; 225-7074
Gulfport: (228) 864-7670
Web Site

Missouri

Rep. William Lacy Clay, Jr. (D-1st)
2418 Rayburn House Office Building
(202) 225-2406; 226-3717
St. Louis: (314) 367-1970
Web Site

Rep. Ann Wagner (R-2nd) **
435 Cannon House Office Building
(202) 225-1621; 225-2563
Ballwin: (636) 779-5449
Web Site

Rep. Blaine Luetkemeyer (R-3rd)
1740 Longworth House Office Building
(202) 225-2956; 225-5712
Columbia: (573) 443-1041
Web Site

Rep. Vicky Hartzler (R-4th)
1023 Longworth House Office Building
(202) 225-2876; 225-0148
Jefferson City: (573) 634-4884
Web Site

Missouri cont.

Rep. Emanuel Cleaver, II (D-5th)
1433 Longworth House Office Building
(202) 225-4535; 225-4403
Kansas City: (816) 842-4545
Web Site

Rep. Sam Graves (R-6th)
1415 Longworth House Office Building
(202) 225-7041; 225-8221
Liberty: (816) 792-3976
Web Site

Rep. Billy Long (R-7th)
1541 Longworth House Office Building
(202) 225-6536; 225-5604
Springfield: (417) 889-1800
Web Site

Rep. Jo Ann Emerson (R-8th)
2230 Rayburn House Office Building
(202) 225-4404; 226-0326
Cape Girardeau: (573) 335-0101
Web Site

Montana

Rep. Steve Daines (R-AL) **
206 Cannon House Office Building
(202) 225-3211; 225-5687
Billings: (406) 969-1736
Web Site

Nebraska

Rep. Jeff Fortenberry (R-1st)
1514 Longworth House Office Building
(202) 225-4806; 225-5686
Lincoln: (402) 438-1598
Web Site

Rep. Lee Terry (R-2nd)
2331 Rayburn House Office Building
(202) 225-4155; 226-5452
Omaha: (402) 397-9944

Nebraska cont.

Rep. Adrian Smith (R-3rd)
503 Cannon House Office Building
(202) 225-6435; 225-0207
Scottsbluff: (308) 633-3333
Web Site

Nevada

Rep. Dina Titus (D-1st) **
401 Cannon House Office Building
(202) 225-5965; 225-3119
Las Vegas: (702) 220-9823
Web Site

Rep. Mark Amodei (R-2nd)
125 Cannon House Office Building
(202) 225-6155; 225-5679
Reno: (775) 686-5760
Web Site

Rep. Joe Heck (R-3rd)
132 Cannon House Office Building
(202) 225-3252; 225-2185
Las Vegas: (702) 387-4941
Web Site

Rep. Steven Horsford (D-4th) **
1330 Longworth House Office Building
(202) 225-9894; 225-9783
N. Las Vegas: (702) 802-4500
Web Site

New Hampshire

Rep. Carol Shea-Porter (D-1st) **
1530 Longworth House Office Building
(202) 225-5456; 225-5822
Manchester: (603) 641-9536
Web Site

Rep. Ann McLane Kuster (D-2nd) **
137 Cannon House Office Building
(202) 225-5206; 225-2946
Concord (603) 226-1002

New Jersey

Rep. Robert Andrews (D-1st)
2265 Rayburn House Office Building
(202) 225-6501; 225-6583
Haddon Heights: (856) 546-5100
Web Site

Rep. Frank LoBiondo (R-2nd)
2427 Rayburn House Office Building
(202) 225-6572; 225-3318
Mays Landing: (800) 471-4450
Web Site

Rep. Jon Runyan (R-3rd)
1239 Longworth House Office Building
(202) 225-4765; 225-0778
Mount Laurel: (856) 780-6436
Web Site

Rep. Christopher Smith (R-4th)
2373 Rayburn House Office Building
(202) 225-3765; 225-7768
Hamilton: (609) 585-7878
Web Site

Rep. Scott Garrett (R-5th)
2244 Rayburn House Office Building
(202) 225-4465; 225-9048
Newton: (973) 300-2000
Web Site

Rep. Frank Pallone, Jr. (D-6th)
237 Cannon House Office Building
(202) 225-4671; 225-9665
Long Branch: (732) 571-1140
Web Site

Rep. Leonard Lance (R-7th)
426 Cannon House Office Building
(202) 225-5361; 225-9460
Westfield: (908) 518-7733
Web Site

Rep. Albio Sires (D-8th)
2342 Rayburn House Office Building
(202) 225-7919; 226-0792
Jersey City: (201) 222-2828
Web Site

New Jersey cont.

Rep. Bill Pascrell, Jr. (D-9th)
2370 Rayburn House Office Building
(202) 225-5751; 225-5782
Paterson: (973) 523-5152
Web Site

Rep. Donald Payne (D-10th)
2310 Rayburn House Office Building
(202) 225-3436; 225-4160
Newark: (973) 645-3213
Web Site

Rep. Rodney Frelinghuysen (R-11th)
2369 Rayburn House Office Building
(202) 225-5034; 225-3186
Morristown: (973) 984-0711
Web Site

Rep. Rush Holt (D-12th)
1214 Longworth House Office Building
(202) 225-5801; 225-6025
West Windsor: (609) 750-9365
Web Site

New Mexico

Rep. Lujan Grisham (D-1st) **
214 Cannon House Office Building
(202) 225-6316; 225-4975
Albuquerque: (505) 346-6781
Web Site

Rep. Steve Pearce (R-2nd)
2432 Rayburn House Office Building
(202) 225-2365; 225-9599
Las Cruces: (855) 473-2723
Web Site

Rep. Ben R. Lujan (D-3rd)
502 Cannon House Office Building
(202) 225-6190; 226-1528
Santa Fe: (505) 984-8950
Web Site

New York

Rep. Tim Bishop (D-1st)
306 Cannon House Office Building
(202) 225-3826; 225-3143
Coram: (631) 696-6500
Web Site

Rep. Peter King (R-2nd)
339 Cannon House Office Building
(202) 225-7896; 226-2279
Massapequa Park: (516) 541-4225
Web Site

Rep. Steve Israel (D-3rd)
2457 Rayburn House Office Building
(202) 225-3335; 225-4669
Hauppauge: (631) 951-2210
Web Site

Rep. Carolyn McCarthy (D-4th)
2346 Rayburn House Office Building
(202) 225-5516; 225-5758
Garden City: (516) 739-3008
Web Site

Rep. Gregory Meeks (D-5th)
2234 Rayburn House Office Building
(202) 225-3461; 226-4169
Far Rockaway: (718) 327-9791
Web Site

Rep. Grace Meng (D-6th) **
1317 Longworth House Office Building
(202) 225-2601; 225-1598
Bayside: (718) 423-2154
Web Site

Rep. Nydia Velazquez (D-7th)
2302 Rayburn House Office Building
(202) 225-2361; 226-0327
Brooklyn: (718) 599-3658
Web Site

Rep. Hakeem Jeffries (D-8th) **
1339 Longworth House Office Building
(202) 225-5936; 225-1018
Brooklyn: (718) 373-0033
Web Site

New York cont.

Rep. Yvette Clarke (D-9th)
1029 Longworth House Office Building
(202) 225-6231; 226-0112
Brooklyn: (718) 287-1142
Web Site

Rep. Jerrold Nadler (D-10th)
2334 Rayburn House Office Building
(202) 225-5635; 225-6923
New York: (212) 367-7350
Web Site

Rep. Mike Grimm (R-11th)
521 Cannon House Office Building
(202) 225-3371; 226-1272
Staten Island: (718) 351-1062
Web Site

Rep. Carolyn Maloney (D-12th)
2332 Rayburn House Office Building
(202) 225-7944; 225-4709
New York: (212) 860-0606
Web Site

Rep. Charles Rangel (D-13th)
2354 Rayburn House Office Building
(202) 225-4365; 225-0816
New York: (212) 663-3900
Web Site

Rep. Joseph Crowley (D-14th)
2404 Rayburn House Office Building
(202) 225-3965; 225-1909
Jackson Heights: (718) 779-1400
Web Site

Rep. Jose Serrano (D-15th)
2227 Rayburn House Office Building
(202) 225-4361; 225-6001
Bronx: (718) 620-0084
Web Site

Rep. Eliot Engel (D-16th)
2161 Rayburn House Office Building
(202) 225-2464; 225-5513
Bronx: (718) 796-9700
Web Site

New York cont.

Rep. Nita Lowey (D-17th)
2365 Rayburn House Office Building
(202) 225-6506; 225-0546
White Plains: (914) 428-1707
Web Site

Rep. Sean Patrick Maloney (D-18th) **
1529 Longworth House Office Building
(202) 225-5441; 225-3289
Fishkill: (845) 202-0563
Web Site

Rep. Christopher Gibson (R-19th)
502 Cannon House Office Building
(202) 225-5614; 225-1168
Glens Falls: (518) 743-0964
Web Site

Rep. Paul Tonko (D-20th)
422 Cannon House Office Building
(202) 225-5076; 225-5077
Albany: (518) 465-0700
Web Site

Rep. Bill Owens (D-21st)
431 Cannon House Office Building
(202) 225-4611; 226-0621
Watertown: (315) 782-3150
Web Site

Rep. Richard Hanna (R-22nd)
319 Cannon House Office Building
(202) 225-3665; 225-1891
Utica: (315) 724-9740
Web Site

Rep. Thomas Reed (R-23rd)
1037 Longworth House Office Building
(202) 225-3161; 226-6599
Pittsford: 585-218-0040
Web Site

Rep. Daniel Maffei (D-24th) **
422 Cannon House Office Building
(202) 225-3701; 225-4042
Auburn: N/A
Web Site

New York cont.

Rep. Louise Slaughter (D-25th)
2469 Rayburn House Office Building
(202) 225-3615; 225-7822
Rochester: (716) 232-4850
Web Site

Rep. Brian Higgins (D-26th)
2459 Rayburn House Office Building
(202) 225-3306; 226-0347
Buffalo: (716) 852-3501
Web Site

Rep. Chris Collins (R-27th) **
1711 Longworth House Office Building
(202) 225-5265; 225-5910
Williamsville: (716) 634-2324
Web Site

North Carolina

Rep. G. K. Butterfield (D-1st)
2305 Rayburn House Office Building
(202) 225-3101; 225-3354
Weldon: (252) 538-4123
Web Site

Rep. Renee Ellmers (R-2nd)
1533 Longworth House Office Building
(202) 225-4531; 225-5662
Dunn: (910) 230-1910
Web Site

Rep. Walter Jones (R-3rd)
2333 Rayburn House Office Building
(202) 225-3415; 225-3286
Greenville: (800) 351-1697
Web Site

Rep. David Price (D-4th)
2162 Rayburn House Office Building
(202) 225-1784; 225-2014
Raleigh: (919) 859-5999
Web Site

North Carolina cont.

Rep. Virginia Foxx (R-5th)
1230 Longworth House Office Building
(202) 225-2071; 225-2995
Clemmons: (336) 778-0211
Web Site

Rep. Howard Coble (R-6th)
2118 Rayburn House Office Building
(202) 225-3065; 225-8611
Greensboro: (336) 333-5005
Web Site

Rep. Mike McIntyre (D-7th)
2133 Rayburn House Office Building
(202) 225-2731; 225-5773
Fayetteville: (910) 323-0260
Web Site

Rep. Richard Hudson (D-8th) **
429 Cannon House Office Building
(202) 225-3715; 225-4036
Concord: (704) 786-1612
Web Site

Rep. Robert Pittenger (R-9th) **
224 Cannon House Office Building
(202) 225-1976; 225-3389
Charlotte: (704) 365-6234
Web Site

Rep. Patrick McHenry (R-10th)
224 Cannon House Office Building
(202) 225-2576; 225-0316
Hickory: (828) 327-6100
Web Site

Rep. Mark Meadows (R-11th) **
1516 Longworth House Office Building
(202) 225-6401; 226-6422
Hendersonville: (828) 693-5660
Web Site

Rep. Melvin Watt (D-12th)
2304 Rayburn House Office Building
(202) 225-1510; 225-1512
Charlotte: (704) 344-9950
Web Site

North Carolina cont.

Rep. George Holding (R-13th) **
507 Cannon House Office Building
(202) 225-3032; 225-0181
Raleigh: (919) 856-9778
Web Site

North Dakota

Rep. Kevin Cramer (R-AL) **
1032 Longworth House Office Building
(202) 225-2611; 226-0893
Bismarck: N/A
Web Site

Ohio

Rep. Steve Chabot (R-1st)
2351 Rayburn House Office Building
(202) 225-2216; 225-3012
Cincinnati: (513) 684-2723
Web Site

Rep. Brad Wenstrup (R-2nd) **
1223 Longworth House Office Building
(202) 225-3164; 225-1992
Cincinnati: (513) 474-7777
Web Site

Rep. Joyce Beatty (D-3rd) **
417 Cannon House Office Building
(202) 225-6465; 225-6754
Columbus: (614) 220-0003
Web Site

Rep. Jim Jordan (R-4th)
1524 Longworth House Office Building
(202) 225-2676; 226-0577
Mansfield: (419) 522-5757
Web Site

Rep. Robert Latta (R-5th)
1323 Longworth House Office Building
(202) 225-6405; 225-1985
Norwalk: (419) 668-0206
Web Site

Ohio cont.

Rep. Bill Johnson (R-6th)
317 Cannon House Office Building
(202) 225-5705; 225-5907
Marietta: (740) 376-0868
Web Site

Rep. Bob Gibbs (R-7th)
329 Cannon House Office Building
(202) 225-6265; 225-3394
Zanesville: (740) 452-2279
Web Site

Rep. John Boehner (R-8th)
1011 Longworth House Office Building
(202) 225-6205; 225-0704
West Chester: (513) 779-5400
Web Site

Rep. Marcy Kaptur (D-9th)
2186 Rayburn House Office Building
(202) 225-4146; 225-7711
Toledo: (419) 259-7500
Web Site

Rep. Michael Turner (R-10th)
2454 Rayburn House Office Building
(202) 225-6465; 225-6754
Dayton: (937) 225-2843
Web Site

Rep. Marcia Fudge (D-11th)
1019 Longworth House Office Building
(202) 225-7032; 225-1339
Warrensville: (216) 522-4900
Web Site

Rep. Patrick Tiberi (R-12th)
106 Cannon House Office Building
(202) 225-5355; 226-4523
Columbus: (614) 523-2555
Web Site

Rep. Tim Ryan (D-13th)
1421 Longworth House Office Building
(202) 225-5261; 225-3719
Youngstown: (330) 740-0193
Web Site

Ohio cont.

Rep. David Joyce (R-14th) **
1535 Longworth House Office Building
(202) 225-5731; 225-3307
Painesville: (440) 352-3939
Web Site

Rep. Steve Stivers (R-15th)
1007 Longworth House Office Building
(202) 225-2015; 225-3529
Columbus: (614) 299-6415
Web Site

Rep. Jim Renacci (R-16th)
130 Cannon House Office Building
(202) 225-3876; 225-3059
Canton: 330-489-4414
Web Site

Oklahoma

Rep. Jim Bridenstine (R-1st) **
216 Cannon House Office Building
(202) 225-2211; 225-9187
Tulsa: (918) 935-3222
Web Site

Rep. Markwayne Mullin (R-2nd) **
1113 Longworth House Office Building
(202) 225-2701; 225-3038
Claremore: (918) 341-9336
Web Site

Rep. Frank Lucas (R-3rd)
2311 Rayburn House Office Building
(202) 225-5565; 225-8698
Yukon: (405) 373-1958
Web Site

Rep. Tom Cole (R-4th)
2458 Rayburn House Office Building
(202) 225-6165; 225-3512
Norman: (405) 329-6500
Web Site

Oklahoma cont.

Rep. James Lankford (R-5th)
509 Cannon House Office Building
(202) 225-2132; 226-1463
Oklahoma City: (405) 234-9900
Web Site

Oregon

Rep. Suzanne Bonamici (D-1st)
2338 Rayburn House Office Building
(202) 225-0855; 225-9497
Portland: (800) 422-4003
Web Site

Rep. Greg Walden (R-2nd)
2182 Rayburn House Office Building
(202) 225-6730; 225-5774
Medford: (800) 533-3303
Web Site

Rep. Earl Blumenauer (D-3rd)
1502 Longworth House Office Building
(202) 225-4811; 225-8941
Portland: (503) 231-2300
Web Site

Rep. Peter DeFazio (D-4th)
2134 Rayburn House Office Building
(202) 225-6416; 226-3493
Eugene: (541) 465-6732
Web Site

Rep. Kurt Schrader (D-5th)
314 Cannon House Office Building
(202) 225-5711; 225-5699
Salem: (503) 588-9100
Web Site

Pennsylvania

Rep. Robert Brady (D-1st)
102 Cannon House Office Building
(202) 225-4731; 225-0088
Philadelphia: (215) 389-4627

Pennsylvania cont.

Rep. Chaka Fattah (D-2nd)
2301 Rayburn House Office Building
(202) 225-4001; 225-5392
Philadelphia: (215) 387-6404
Web Site

Rep. Mike Kelly (R-3rd)
515 Cannon House Office Building
(202) 225-5406; 225-3103
Erie: (814) 454-8190
Web Site

Rep. Scott Perry (R-4th) **
126 Cannon House Office Building
(202) 225-5836; 226-1000
Gettysburg: (717) 338-1919
Web Site

Rep. Glenn Thompson (R-5th)
124 Cannon House Office Building
(202) 225-5121; 225-5796
Bellefonte: (814) 353-0215
Web Site

Rep. Jim Gerlach (R-6th)
2442 Rayburn House Office Building
(202) 225-4315; 225-8440
Wyomissing: (610) 376-7630
Web Site

Rep. Patrick Meehan (R-7th)
513 Cannon House Office Building
(202) 225-2011; 226-0280
Springfield: (610) 690-7323
Web Site

Rep. Michael Fitzpatrick (R-8th)
1224 Longworth House Office Building
(202) 225-4276; 225-9511
Langhome: (215) 579-8102
Web Site

Rep. Bill Shuster (R-9th)
204 Cannon House Office Building
(202) 225-2431; 225-2486
Chambersburg: (717) 264-8308
Web Site

Pennsylvania cont.

Rep. Thomas Marino (R-10th)
410 Cannon House Office Building
(202) 225-3731; 225-9594
Williamsport: (570) 322-3961
Web Site

Rep. Lou Barletta (R-11th)
115 Cannon House Office Building
(202) 225-6511; 226-6250
Hazelton: (570) 751-0050
Web Site

Rep. Keith Rothfus (R-12th) **
503 Cannon House Office Building
(202) 225-2065; 225-5709
Pittsburgh: (412) 837-1361
Web Site

Rep. Allyson Schwartz (D-13th)
1227 Longworth House Office Building
(202) 225-6111; 226-0611
Philadelphia: (215) 335-3355
Web Site

Rep. Mike Doyle (D-14th)
401 Cannon House Office Building
(202) 225-2135; 225-3084
Penn Hills: (412) 241-6055
Web Site

Rep. Charles Dent (R-15th)
1009 Longworth House Office Building
(202) 225-6411; 226-0778
Bethlehem: (610) 861-9734
Web Site

Rep. Joseph Pitts (R-16th)
420 Cannon House Office Building
(202) 225-2411; 225-2013
Lancaster: (717) 393-0667
Web Site

Rep. Matthew Cartwright (D-17th) **
1419 Longworth House Office Building
(202) 225-5546; 226-0996
Scranton: (570) 341-1050
Web Site

Pennsylvania cont.

Rep. Tim Murphy (R-18th)
322 Cannon House Office Building
(202) 225-2301; 225-1844
Pittsburgh: (412) 344-5583

Puerto Rico

Res. Com. Pedro Pierluisi (D-AL)
1218 Longworth House Office Building
(202) 225-2615; 225-2154
Old San Juan: (787) 723-6333
Web Site

Rhode Island

Rep. David Cicilline (D-1st)
128 Cannon House Office Building
(202) 225-4911; 225-3290
Pawtucket: (401) 729-5600
Web Site

Rep. James Langevin (D-2nd)
109 Cannon House Office Building
(202) 225-2735; 225-5976
Warwick: (401) 732-9400
Web Site

South Carolina

Rep. VACANT (-1st) **
Special Election May 17, 2013
322 Cannon House Office Building
(202) 225-3176; 225-3407
N/A
Web Site

Rep. Joe Wilson (R-2nd)
2229 Rayburn House Office Building
(202) 225-2452; 225-2455
Beaufort: (843) 521-2530
Web Site

Rep. Jeff Duncan (R-3rd)
116 Cannon House Office Building
(202) 225-5301; 225-3216
Anderson: (864) 224-7401

South Carolina cont.

Rep. Trey Gowdy (R-4th)
1237 Longworth House Office Building
(202) 225-6030; 226-1177
Greenville: (864) 241-0175
Web Site

Rep. Mick Mulvaney (R-5th)
1004 Longworth House Office Building
(202) 225-5501; 225-0464
Rock Hill: (803) 327-1114
Web Site

Rep. James Clyburn (D-6th)
2135 Rayburn House Office Building
(202) 225-3315; 225-2313
Columbia: (803) 799-1100
Web Site

Rep. Tom Rice, Jr. (R-7th) **
325 Cannon House Office Building
(202) 225-9895; 225-9690
Myrtle Beach: (843) 445-6459
Web Site

South Dakota

Rep. Kristi Noem (R-AL)
226 Cannon House Office Building
(202) 225-2801; 225-5823
Sioux Falls: (605) 275-2868
Web Site

Tennessee

Rep. Phil Roe (R-1st)
419 Cannon House Office Building
(202) 225-6356; 225-5714
Morristown: (423) 254-1400
Web Site

Rep. John Duncan, Jr. (R-2nd)
2207 Rayburn House Office Building
(202) 225-5435; 225-6440
Knoxville: (423) 523-3772
Web Site

Tennessee cont.

Rep. Chuck Fleischmann (R-3rd)
511 Cannon House Office Building
(202) 225-3271; 225-3494
Chattanooga: (423) 756-2342
Web Site

Rep. Scott DesJarlais (R-4th)
413 Cannon House Office Building
(202) 225-6831; 226-5172
Columbia: (931) 381-9920
Web Site

Rep. Jim Cooper (D-5th)
1536 Longworth House Office Building
(202) 225-4311; 226-1035
Nashville: (615) 736-5295
Web Site

Rep. Diane Black (R-6th)
1531 Longworth House Office Building
(202) 225-4231; 225-6887
Murfreesboro: (615) 896-1986
Web Site

Rep. Marsha Blackburn (R-7th)
217 Cannon House Office Building
(202) 225-2811; 225-3004
Memphis: (901) 382-5811
Web Site

Rep. Stephen Fincher (R-8th)
1118 Longworth House Office Building
(202) 225-4714; 225-1765
Jackson: (731) 423-4848
Web Site

Rep. Steve Cohen (D-9th)
1005 Longworth House Office Building
(202) 225-3265; 225-5663
Memphis: (901) 544-4131
Web Site

Texas

Rep. Louie Gohmert (R-1st)
2440 Rayburn House Office Building
(202) 225-3035; 226-1230
Tyler: (903) 561-6349
Web Site

Rep. Ted Poe (R-2nd)
430 Cannon House Office Building
(202) 225-6565; 225-5547
Beaumont: (877) 218-1997
Web Site

Rep. Sam Johnson (R-3rd)
1211 Longworth House Office Building
(202) 225-4201; 225-1485
Richardson: (972) 470-0892
Web Site

Rep. Ralph Hall (R-4th)
2405 Rayburn House Office Building
(202) 225-6673; 225-3332
Rockwall: (972) 771-9118
Web Site

Rep. Jeb Hensarling (R-5th)
129 Cannon House Office Building
(202) 225-3484; 225-4888
Dallas: (214) 349-9996
Web Site

Rep. Joe Barton (R-6th)
2109 Rayburn House Office Building
(202) 225-2002; 225-3052
Arlington: (817) 543-1000
Web Site

Texas cont.

Rep. John Culberson (R-7th)
2352 Rayburn House Office Building
(202) 225-2571; 225-4381
Houston: (713) 682-8828
Web Site

Rep. Kevin Brady (R-8th)
301 Cannon House Office Building
(202) 225-4901; 225-5524
Conroe: (936) 441-5700
Web Site

Rep. Al Green (D-9th)
2201 Rayburn House Office Building
(202) 225-7508; 225-2947
Houston: (713) 383-9234
Web Site

Rep. Michael McCaul (R-10th)
131 Cannon House Office Building
(202) 225-2401; 225-5955
Austin: (512) 473-2357
Web Site

Rep. Mike Conaway (R-11th)
2430 Rayburn House Office Building
(202) 225-3605; 225-1783
Midland: (432) 687-2390
Web Site

Rep. Kay Granger (R-12th)
320 Cannon House Office Building
(202) 225-5071; 225-5683
Ft. Worth: (817) 338-0909
Web Site

Rep. Mac Thornberry (R-13th)
2209 Rayburn House Office Building
(202) 225-3706; 225-3486
Amarillo: (806) 371-8844
Web Site

Rep. Randy Weber (R-14th) *
510 Cannon House Office Building
(202) 225-2831; 225-0271
Lake Jackson: (979) 285-0231
Web Site

Texas cont.

Rep. Ruben Hinojosa (D-15th)
2262 Rayburn House Office Building
(202) 225-2531; 225-5688
McAllen: (956) 682-5545
Web Site

Rep. Beto O'Rourke (D-16th) *
1721 Longworth House Office Building
(202) 225-4831; 225-2016
El Paso: N/A
Web Site

Rep. Bill Flores (R-17th)
1505 Longworth House Office Building
(202) 225-6105; 225-0350
Waco: (254) 732-0748
Web Site

Rep. Sheila Jackson Lee (D-18th)
2160 Rayburn House Office Building
(202) 225-3816; 225-3317
Houston: (713) 655-0050
Web Site

Rep. Randy Neugebauer (R-19th)
1424 Longworth House Office Building
(202) 225-4005; 225-9615
Lubbock: (806) 763-1611
Web Site

Rep. Joaquin Castro (D-20th) *
212 Cannon House Office Building
(202) 225-3236; 225-1915
San Antonio: (210) 348-8216
Web Site

Rep. Lamar Smith (R-21st)
2409 Rayburn House Office Building
(202) 225-4236; 225-8628
San Antonio: (210) 821-5024
Web Site

Rep. Pete Olson (R-22nd)
312 Cannon House Office Building
(202) 225-5951; 225-5241
Sugar Land: (281) 494-2690
Web Site

Texas cont.

Rep. Pete Gallego (D-23rd) **
431 Cannon House Office Building
(202) 225-4511; 225-2237
N/A
Web Site

Rep. Kenny Marchant (R-24th)
1110 Longworth House Office Building
(202) 225-6605; 225-0074
Irving: (972) 556-0162
Web Site

Rep. Roger Williams (R-25th) **
1122 Longworth House Office Building
(202) 225-9896; 225-9692
Austin: (512) 473-8910
Web Site

Rep. Michael Burgess (R-26th)
2241 Rayburn House Office Building
(202) 225-7772; 225-2919
Lewisville: (972) 434-9700
Web Site

Rep. Blake Farenthold (R-27th)
2110 Rayburn House Office Building
(202) 225-7742; 226-1134
Corpus Christi: (361) 884-2222
Web Site

Rep. Henry Cuellar (D-28th)
2463 Rayburn House Office Building
(202) 225-1640; 225-1641
San Antonio: (210) 271-2851
Web Site

Rep. Gene Green (D-29th)
2470 Rayburn House Office Building
(202) 225-1688; 225-9903
Houston: (281) 999-5879
Web Site

Rep. Eddie Bernice Johnson (D-30th)
2468 Rayburn House Office Building
(202) 225-8885; 226-1477
Dallas: (214) 922-8885
Web Site

Texas cont.

Rep. John Carter (R-31st)
409 Cannon House Office Building
(202) 225-3864; 225-5886
Round Rock: (512) 246-1600
Web Site

Rep. Pete Sessions (R-32nd)
2233 Rayburn House Office Building
(202) 225-2231; 225-5878
Dallas: (972) 392-0505
Web Site

Rep. Marc Veasey (D-33rd) **
414 Cannon House Office Building
(202) 225-9897; 225-9702
Dallas: (214) 741-1387
Web Site

Rep. Filemon Vela, Jr. (D-34th) **
437 Cannon House Office Building
(202) 225-9901; 226-0475
Brownsville: (956) 544-8352
Web Site

Rep. Lloyd Doggett (D-35th)
201 Cannon House Office Building
(202) 225-4865; 225-3073
Austin: (512) 916-5921
Web Site

Rep. Steve Stockman (R-36th) **
326 Casnnon House Office Building
(202) 225-1555; 226-0396
Orange: (409) 883-8028
Web Site

Utah

Rep. Rob Bishop (R-1st)
123 Cannon House Office Building
(202) 225-0453; 225-5857
Ogden: (801) 625-0107
Web Site

Rep. Chris Stewart (R-2nd) **
323 Cannon House Office Building
(202) 225-9730; 225-5629
Salt Lake City: (801) 364-5550
Web Site

Rep. Jason Chaffetz (R-3rd)
1032 Longworth House Office Building
(202) 225-7751; 225-5629
Provo: (801) 851-2500
Web Site

Rep. Jim Matheson (D-4th)
2434 Rayburn House Office Building
(202) 225-3011; 225-5638
South Salt Lake: (801) 486-1236
Web Site

Vermont

Rep. Peter Welch (D-AL)
1404 Longworth House Office Building
(202) 225-4115; 225-6790
Burlington: (888) 605-7270
Web Site

Virgin Islands

Del. Donna Christensen (D-AL)
1510 Longworth House Office Building
(202) 225-1790; 225-5517
St. Thomas: (340) 774-4408
Web Site

Virginia

Rep. Robert Wittman (R-1st)
1317 Longworth House Office Building
(202) 225-4261; 225-4382
Yorktown: (757) 874-6687
Web Site

Rep. Scott Rigell (R-2nd)
327 Cannon House Office Building
(202) 225-4215; 225-4218
Virginia Beach: (757) 687-8290
Web Site

Rep. Bobby Scott (D-3rd)
1201 Longworth House Office Building
(202) 225-8351; 225-8354
Newport News: (757) 380-1000
Web Site

Rep. Randy Forbes (R-4th)
2438 Rayburn House Office Building
(202) 225-6365; 226-1170
Chesapeake: (757) 382-0080
Web Site

Rep. Robert Hurt (R-5th)
1516 Longworth House Office Building
(202) 225-4711; 225-5681
Danville: (434) 791-2596
Web Site

Rep. Bob Goodlatte (R-6th)
2240 Rayburn House Office Building
(202) 225-5431; 225-9681
Roanoke: (540) 857-2672
Web Site

Rep. Eric Cantor (R-7th)
303 Cannon House Office Building
(202) 225-2815; 225-0011
Glen Allen: (804) 747-4073
Web Site

Rep. Jim Moran (D-8th)
2239 Rayburn House Office Building
(202) 225-4376; 225-0017
Alexandria: (703) 971-4700
Web Site

Virginia cont.

Rep. Morgan Griffith (R-9th)
1108 Longworth House Office Building
(202) 225-3861; 225-0442
Abingdon: (276) 525-1405
Web Site

Rep. Frank Wolf (R-10th)
241 Cannon House Office Building
(202) 225-5136; 225-0437
Herndon: (800) 945-9653
Web Site

Rep. Gerry Connolly (D-11th)
424 CannonHouse Office Building
(202) 225-1492; 225-3071
Annandale: (703) 256-3071
Web Site

Washington

Rep. Suzan K. DelBene (D-1st) **
318 Cannon House Office Building
(202) 225-6311; 226-1606
Bothell: (425) 485-0085
Web Site

Rep. Rick Larsen (D-2nd)
108 Cannon House Office Building
(202) 225-2605; 225-4420
Everett: (425) 252-3188
Web Site

Rep. Jaime Herrera Beutler (R-3rd)
1130 Longworth House Office Building
(202) 225-3536; 225-3478
Vancouver: (360) 695-6292
Web Site

Rep. Doc Hastings (R-4th)
1203 Longworth House Office Building
(202) 225-5816; 225-3251
Pasco: (509) 543-9396
Web Site

Washington cont.

Rep. Jaime Herrera Beutler (R-3rd)
1130 Longworth House Office Building
(202) 225-3536; 225-3478
Vancouver: (360) 695-6292
Web Site

Rep. Doc Hastings (R-4th)
1203 Longworth House Office Building
(202) 225-5816; 225-3251
Pasco: (509) 543-9396
Web Site

Rep. Cathy McMorris Rodgers (R-5th)
2421 Rayburn House Office Building
(202) 225-2006; 225-3392
Spokane: (509) 353-2374
Web Site

Rep. Derek Kilmer (D-6th) **
1429 Longworth House Office Building
(202) 225-5916; 593-6551
Bremerton: (360) 373-9725
Web Site

Rep. Jim McDermott (D-7th)
1035 Longworth House Office Building
(202) 225-3106; 225-6197
Seattle: (206) 553-7170
Web Site

Rep. David G. Reichert (R-8th)
1730 Longworth House Office Building
(202) 225-7761; 225-4282
Mercer Island: (206) 275-3438
Web Site

Rep. Adam Smith (D-9th)
2402 Rayburn House Office Building
(202) 225-8901; 225-5893
Tacoma: (253) 593-6600
Web Site

Rep. Denny Heck (D-10th) **
425 Cannon House Office Building
(202) 225-9740; 225-0129
Lacey: (360) 459-8514
Web Site

West Virginia

Rep. David McKinley (R-1st)
313 Cannon House Office Building
(202) 225-4172; 225-7564
Wheeling: (304) 232-3801
Web Site

Rep. Shelley Moore Capito (R-2nd)
2443 Rayburn House Office Building
(202) 225-2711; 225-7856
Charleston: (304) 925-5964
Web Site

Rep. Nick Rahall (D-3rd)
2307 Rayburn House Office Building
(202) 225-3452; 225-9061
Beckley: (304) 252-5000
Web Site

Wisconsin

Rep. Paul Ryan (R-1st)
1233 Longworth House Office Building
(202) 225-3031; 225-3393
Janesville: (608) 752-4050
Web Site

Rep. Mark Pocan (D-2nd) **
313 Cannon House Office Building
(202) 225-2906; 225-6942
Madison: (608) 258-9800
Web Site

Rep. Ron Kind (D-3rd)
1406 Longworth House Office Building
(202) 225-5506; 225-5739
La Crosse: (888) 442-8040
Web Site

Rep. Gwen Moore (D-4th)
2245 Rayburn House Office Building
(202) 225-4572; 225-8135
Milwaukee: (414) 297-1140
Web Site

Wisconsin cont.

Rep. F. James Sensenbrenner (R-5th)
2449 Rayburn House Office Building
(202) 225-5101; 225-3190
Brookfield: (414) 784-1111
Web Site

Rep. Thomas Petri (R-6th)
2462 Rayburn House Office Building
(202) 225-2476; 225-2356
Fond du Lac: (800) 242-4883

Rep. Sean Duffy (R-7th)
1208 Longworth House Office Building
(202) 225-3365; 225-3240
Wausau: (715) 298-9344
Web Site

Rep. Reid Ribble (R-8th)
1513 Longworth House Office Building
(202) 225-5665; 225-5729
Appleton: (920) 380-0061
Web Site

Wyoming

Rep. Cynthia Lummis (R-AL)
113 Cannon House Office Building
(202) 225-2311; 225-3057
Cheyenne: (307) 772-2595
Web Site

U.S. House of Representatives

Committees

Administration
Agriculture
Appropriations
Armed Services
Banking
Budget
Commerce
Education & Workforce
Ethics
International Relations
Joint Economic
Joint Taxation
Judiciary
Reform
Resources
Rules
Science
Small Business
Transportation & Infrastructure
Veterans' Affairs
Ways & Means

Acknowledgements
Credits, References, And Sources

Presidents images' courtesy of the U.S. Library of Congress(.gov) per Lora Szypszak, Reference Assistance, Prints and Photographs Division. 7-8837 http://www.loc.gov/rr/print/list/057pral.html

President Donald J. Trump image courtesy of U.S.A. gov image case #01148375-195
https://www.whitehouse.gov/administration/president-trump

All photos and quotes from President Ronald Reagan and First Lady Nancy Reagan are courtesy of Ronald Reagan Library. Steve Branch steve,branch@nara.gov www.reaganlibrary.gov

All Presidents' quotes retrieved from presidential archives courtesy of U.S. Library of Congress (.gov)

Presidential Papers retrieved from U.S. Library of Congress(.gov) https://www.loc.gov.collections

The Federalist papers retrieved https://www.congress.gov/resources/display/content/the+Federalist+papers

Chief Justices' opinions and dissents retrieved https://www.supremecourt.gov

Quote by Charles Darwin retrieved www.pdegraaf.com
https://www.google.com/amp/s/mdharrismd.com/2013/04/29/quotationsasmanfacesdeath/amp

Quote by Dennis Prager retrieved
https://quotes.lifehack.org/by-author/dennisprager/

Quotes by Adolf Hitler and propaganda minister Joseph Goebbels retrieved digital.cjh.org
https://www.jewishvirtuallibrary.org/joseph-goebbels
https://archive.org/details/AdolfHitlerStatements-01-10
https://en.m.wikisource.org/wiki/author!Adolf_Hitler

Quote by Ann Coulter retrieved ADIOS, America
https://archive.org/stream

Continued on next page

Acknowledgements
Credits, References, And Sources cont.

Quote by Carly Fiorina retrieved ABC News July 12, 2015 9:42AM
abcnews.go.com/this week/video/carly-fiorina2016-presidential-
rac-32393061

Quote by Senator John Cornyn retrieved
cnn.com>transcripts> ldt.oo.html

Quote by Richard Engel retrieved Trump inauguration: What the world
is saying about the new president NBC News>story line>inauguration
January 20, 2017 Richard Engel (@ Richard Engel)

Quote by Benjamin Netanyahu Prime Minister of Israel United Nation >
gadebate>files>LL_EN

Quote By Phyllis Schlafly retrieved eagle@eagleforum.org

Quote by Rush Limbaugh retrieved
tunein.com/radio/the-rush-Limbaugh-show-p2017

Thanksgiving Proclamation U.S. Library of Congress(.gov)

Declaration of Independence retrieved
http://www.constitution.org/us_doi.pdf

Constitution of the United States retrieved
U.S. Library of Congress(.gov)

Bill of Rights Simplified derived from
https://users.csc.calpoly.edu/~jdalbey/Public/Bill_of_Rights.html

Bill of Rights retrieved U.S. Library of Congress(.gov)

List of U.S. Senators retrieved https://www.senate.gov/general/contact_
information/senators_cfm.cfm?OrderBy=state&Sort=ASC

List of U.S. Congress retrieved
http://www.theorator.com/government/house.html#alabama

Chipps family photos courtesy of Janet R. Chipps

All public information and documents retrieved from the public domain
therefore not subject to copyright infringement.

www.ingramcontent.com/pod-product-compliance
Lightning Source LLC
Chambersburg PA
CBHW050120280326
41933CB00010B/1180